AF263665

Capable You

About the Author

Everline Aboka is an author, accredited speaker and coach on affirmations and visualizations, self-awareness, integrity, positive thinking, self-esteem, success, dreams, destiny, compassion, passion, optimism, talent utilization, fashion and modelling, child protection, courage, forgiveness, communications, social values and philanthropy. She has mostly coached young and promising individuals in summer camps, learning institutions including universities, corporate events as well as non-profit organizations both in Kenya and Canada on above or related topics.

Everline believes that each and every individual around the globe has all the ability inside him/her to be the epitome of success in all aspect of his/her life. Her passion is to make self-help information available to any individual who is willing to kick out mediocrity from his/her life and usher in an extraordinary life not only to themselves but also to pass down that same information to generations that will live after them.

Apart from writing, speaking and fashion modelling, in 2008 after being announced M-net Face of Africa Finalist, Everline founded HOPE Africa Foundation in Kisumu, Kenya. An organization that is currently reaching out to street children with food and clothing aid. Her big dream for this project is to build a rescue center that will act as a transition home for these children who are often cold, hungry, deprived of love and education

Copyright © 2010 by Everline Aboka

All rights reserved. This book or any portion thereof may not be reproduced or used in any manner whatsoever without the express written permission of the publisher except for the use of brief quotations in a book review. Printed by create space

First Printing, 2015

Edited by Simon Rose

ISBN 978-9948979-0-9

Everline Aboka
Calgary, Alberta
Canada

www.everlineaboka.com

Appreciation

To my loving mother, Anna Awuor Aboka. Thank you very much for finding time out of your busy schedule as a businesswoman to narrate stories to us in our childhood. This certainly helped me to develop my communications skills to be successful in writing this book. You are my eagle and on your wings, I can see beyond the skies. Your prayers, mentorship, love, encouragement and pieces of advice are gems I could never find in any treasure trove, no matter how deeply it were buried.

To my late father, Raphael Aboka McOnyango. Thank you very much for believing in me and planting powerful and beautiful seed of confidence in my life. This confidence in my abilities has always been appreciated wherever I've traveled in the world. Your love, mentorship, and sheer presence in my life for the short 15 years we spent together were all truly remarkable.

To my best friend and husband Norbert Griess. Thank you very much for being a true heart and lifelong friend for all the years I've known you. You've stood by my side while in pursuit of my dreams and I hope that I'm able to do the same for you, now and always.

To my siblings, Nicholas Aboka, Charles Aboka, Erickson Sunday Aboka, Risper Tracey Aboka, Lilian Aboka, and Frankline Aboka. Your constant support, love, and concern for my dreams are the fuel for my engine. I simply cannot move forward without you. You bless my heart, and I love you all

To my mentors and friends, Bishop Mark Kegohi, Hon. Otieno McOnyango, Hon. Olago Aluoch, Linus Oluma, Syprose Oluma, Eunice Dola, Lilian Obada Oloo , Caroline Ogot, Job Owuor, Peter Ochieng, Patience Dali and the Watiti's. Thank you very much for devoting your time to influence my life through your pieces of advice, encouragement and guidance. You are the torch that rekindles this fire within my soul.

To all my nieces and nephews, fans in Kenya and abroad, members of HOPE Africa Foundation, Tuungane Youth Projects, Elegant Ladies and Christ campaigners Kisumu. You are all the reason I keep pushing higher and higher. Thank you for your constant love and support.

To Phil Cozier, Patrick Luu, Kat Leto, Jason Mellor and Benish Khan, thank you very very much for investing so much of your talents that has made the final outcome of this book be this spectacular! You are the best team I will recommend to anyone.

To my esteemed readers thank you for choosing this book as a self-help tool for your life, I hope you encounter your ''Capable You'' as you read through.

Contents

Introduction

As children we're very enthusiastic about life and our dreams. We know that we want to become a doctor, a lawyer, a teacher, a fashion model, a fire fighter, a writer, a movie star, and all those other job titles that we've all heard children proclaim they want to achieve when they grow up. As children, these dreams become so strong and special to us that we repeat them to our parents, relatives, teachers, friends, and even strangers. We're convinced that we can make it and nothing can stop us but not until that same teacher, parent, friend, or stranger slams our dreams in our faces and tells us that we can't reach our goals. That always hits us so hard and becomes a lethal threat to our dream systems. Before we know it, just like a computer affected by a deadly virus, we start experiencing massive and negative infection in our brain software or even a total crash of our entire dream big software, unless we consider reprogramming the damaged brain system to protect our entire body software from contamination, we are headed for a total software degradation that could lead to life of mediocrity.

Daisy

Growing up, Daisy was a very focused and ambitious girl. She knew in her heart that she wanted to grow up to be a successful and extraordinary musical artist. She loved singing and writing songs. When she was eight years old, Daisy led her school in the singing of the national anthem to mark the beginning of summer games in her province. She gave it her best and received great applause from the audience. Unfortunately when she and her team returned backstage after what they considered to be an excellent performance, Daisy's music teacher scolded her for singing one line in a very high note that almost choked the whole choir. Daisy didn't realize that she'd made this mistake and neither did her friends that had joined her in singing the national anthem. Daisy, a sweet and talented young girl that had been enthusiastically applauded by others, was scolded by the teacher immediately following her performance. Daisy's teacher went on to tell her that as long as he remained her music teacher, she'd never be given another chance to lead the choir in any event. Daisy thought that because she'd sung the national anthem so well the music teacher would be proud of her but that wasn't the case. The words of the music teacher that day contaminated this little girl's dream to sing and possibly get awards in the future.

Daisy's parents, Charles and Judith, were among those that were honoured to see their daughter's impressive and historic performance at the summer games kick-off. They were extremely proud of their little girl. At the conclusion of the event, they joined Daisy and couldn't stop reminding her how proud they were of her. However, Daisy didn't look happy, despite all the compliments. Even though she didn't tell her parents that the teacher had scolded her, her parents soon noticed that Daisy didn't want to run to her music room to learn new keys on her piano anymore. Days turned into weeks, then into months, then the months became years but Daisy didn't go to her music classes nor touch any of her musical instruments at home. She'd been told she wasn't good and so decided to give up on her passion. Fortunately, one day Daisy decided to tell her parents what the teacher had told her and that the teacher was the reason why she'd quit music because she told her she wasn't good enough. Her parents were surprised at this and immediately started a mission to get Daisy to take up music again. They believed that Daisy was capable of much than a simple mistake in a higher key in one line of an entire national anthem. They believed that the incident was merely part of a learning process for their little girl and shouldn't be used to disconnect Daisy from her destiny

After a few months of encouragement from her parents, Daisy returned to singing and song writing after abandoning her passion for two years, She not only recovered her lost passion. Her parents transferred her to a better music and arts school where her talent was appreciated. Before long Daisy was winning awards in both local and international school musical competitions. Today, Daisy has many awards to her credit and has become a successful businesswoman, running a music school in her province with exceptional music production services. She found her passion, followed it, and she's now offering other people the opportunity to sing and follow their passion too.

Chapter One
That Capable You

In this first chapter of this book, we'll look at ways in which we can identify those specific talents that might direct us to a successful career and the type of life that we all dream of. Most of the observations in this chapter have helped many people find their passions in life, including those that never believed that they possessed any special gifts or talents.

You are capable

Just like Daisy and many others, you too are capable of achieving your dreams and making a difference. We may not all end up as successful singers like Daisy but we can build our dreams because each and every individual alive on the face of earth today has at least one unique talent. The ability to do anything lies within us. All that we need to ask ourselves is whether we know and believe that this ability exists.

So many people endure lives of mediocrity when they should be experiencing their dream lives.

Our responsibility in life is to live the life of our dreams not the life that someone else has dreamed or presented to us. We're not what people say we are, so why should we live the kind of life that they deem to be suitable for us? At some point in your life somebody might have told you that you were a loser or a failure, know that doesn't mean that you should live the life of a loser or a failure. *Failing and losing are aspects of everyone's life and they should never embody an individual's identity.* Rise up and banish those negative words and remarks from your system. Begin reprogramming your mind with the positive words that will help you rebuild your life's dreams and lead you on the path to a positive life.

How to know your capabilities

Every time before I travel, I plan my trips and take care of necessities, such as airline tickets, accommodation, travel insurance, and so on before I embark on my trip. The same principles apply to our capabilities or talents. We can't start chasing after them until we know what they are. If we fail do so, we find ourselves running after everything and we all know how unsuccessful it can be to simultaneously pursue many targets. If we chase too many things, the chances are that we won't catch any of them. Yet if we chase one thing at a time we're often more likely to achieve better results. The following guidelines examine some of the ways in which you can determine your unique talents.

The things that you love to do
People often are confused about the definition of talent. Many people think that talent involves only artistic endeavours, such as singing or dancing. However talent is best defined as that in which you excel in and also love to do. For example, your talent could be teaching, based on the fact that you not only love to read and gather information but also love to share the same knowledge with others.

Anna and Tracy

Anna and Tracy again five years after their high school graduation when they both randomly moved into a new city. After a long time without seeing one another, it seems magical to them that they both work for the same company and were just recently transferred to this new city that reconnects them in again but even in a much bigger and special way. They both realised that they needed to engage in a few activities that they could do in the summer that were similar to those they'd experienced in high school. Even though Anna and Tracy enjoyed many similar activities in high school, such as swimming, cheerleading, debating, and acting, they both realized that neither of them truly loved participating in these. Their parents had always pushed them into such activities in order to keep them busy, few of their classmates are currently breaking records as swimmers, politicians and movie stars but not Anna and Tracy. They've ended up working for a large technology company as software programmers in their new city.

Anna and Tracy both have a three-month holiday each summer to spend together. The two ladies embarked on a journey to discover activities that they could not only excel in but also love to do, so that they could stay active, relaxed and focused in the summer. After trying separate activities, they both realised that cycling was one of the things that they each loved to do and could excel in without getting pushed by anyone. They started riding their bicycles to and from work together five days a week. They also registered for a cyclist's race in the city later that summer and finished in first and third place respectively. Today Anna and Tracy know that their talent lies in cycling, an activity that they both love. Interestingly, cycling is also an activity which their parents didn't consider even though they taught them how to ride the tricycles and bicycles that they received as gifts when they were children. Just like Anna and Tracy, you can find your talents hidden in the things that you love by trying various activities that you possibly even tried earlier in your life but never pursued for a long time. *A talent is within you can never die. You can rekindle it when you begin to pursue it again with real passion and purpose.*

Observations about you by family, friends, and strangers

Although this is a complex guide to follow when attempting to determine your talents and passions, considering it involves other people's observations about you, it's important to remember that what others see in us is very often not what we see ourselves. However, this strategy can still help to lead you to an activity that you like to do but had never considered to be a talent, even though you're skilled at it and love to do it. Sometimes others can observe what we don't see, so be humble enough to accept other people's observations since these can guide you to achieving your goals. If you realize that such observations from others are mainly negative observations that are in conflict with what you already know about yourself, don't hesitate, feel free to politely dismiss these opinions and build on your current knowledge about yourself.

My parents invested so much in my modelling career, especially my late father, Raphael Aboka. I was born when he was out of town and he was so happy that he finally had a girl in his family. I became his princess and he became my king. We had a very strong father-daughter relationship and enjoyed many moments together. Despite the bond, I don't remember a time when my father referred to me by my names. To him I was more than a name written on a birth certificate, a name I acquired in his absence, so he felt or even thought. He saw beyond Everline and instead called me ''*nyarber*'' (beauty) all his life. Fate unfortunately decreed that we only spent the first 15 years of my life together. Yet there's a part of me that believes that my confidence to strut the global runway is strongly connected to how my father built such a powerful foundation for my career through his words that have resurfaced everywhere I've traveled.

My family, high school teachers, and friends soon started to see my capability to shine in the fashion industry as a model. I can still remember the words of

Mrs. Loyce Wadeya, one of my teachers in high school.

"Girl," she said. "You can make a very successful model."

I was a typical shy girl when I was growing up, so I simply thanked her and walked away, never thinking of it again. All I knew was that writing was my talent and that was it. On another occasion I met a complete stranger on the streets of Kisumu, a small town in Kenya. The woman told me that I looked like a Face of Africa model. I knew of this modelling competition so I felt good about her comment. Later that same year the Face of Africa competition called for model auditions in Nairobi, Kenya. I was selected among thousands of hopeful models as the only Kenyan finalist. I represented my country in the competition that brought together girls from many other African nations for the honour to be named Face of Africa 2008. I've come to realize that I'm a woman that makes heads turn and people stop me on the street to compliment me on my beauty. I know that I didn't make myself beautiful and that it was God's work and my dad backed it up with powerful

Capable You –Everline Aboka   [20]

words. Today I'm enjoying the one thing that's given me so much exposure in the worldwide fashion industry. Because my dad always called me beauty, I was confident enough to pursue a fashion career in an industry dominated by beautiful girls many years later despite growing up a shy girl. And without my family, friends, and teachers constantly reminding me that I could make it, I wouldn't have even thought about it, let alone attempt to forge a career. Consequently, I'm a firm believer in the power of the observations of family, friends, and strangers to help us to discover our hidden talents and passions.

Learn new things

As we grow older our fear of trying out new things intensifies. We'd rather stick to the status quo and believe that change is not something that we'd enjoy in most cases, that is if we ever enjoy it at all.

''Success is for those who know that whatever way they decide to move they can make it, they are not afraid to crawl, walk or even run to success. They

understand that any kind of motion will take them there anyway.''

''Every learning process involves stages. Think of yourself as a little baby that's learning to walk for the first time when you consider pursuing a certain activity in order to realise your gifts and potential. You'll have moments when you try to stand but still wobble. You'll then move past that and take the first, second, and even third step although you might still find yourself wobbling occasionally. Learning to stand up again is the most important aspect of your struggle to achieve your end results and goals, which in this case is walking upright and steadily maintaining a normal walking pace and posture.''

When I decided to start pursuing modelling, it seemed like something I wouldn't enjoy in my teenage years but I gave it a try and it worked out well. I was lucky to get a scholarship from Mrs. Owino of *ex-elle* to study modelling and fashion at Beauty and Fashion School. This really helped to boost my confidence and prepare me for my time in the fashion industry, even though my feet and back hurt so much from catwalk training when I started. I pushed through the full-time six months training period and gained all the knowledge I needed to get me started as a professional model.

Nicholas and George

These two young men were not only neighbours but also attended school and did their post school hours studies together. It was the first school holiday after these two teenagers had joined high school when they were walking from the community library that they noticed a strange man was approaching them. The man had noticed that the boys were tall, fit, and strong. The man told them that he'd been coaching basketball teams in the city but was also sending students abroad should they desire to study outside the country. Nicholas and George knew about basketball but it wasn't something that they'd considered getting involved in, considering it wasn't a popular sport in the slums of Nyalenda, Kisumu, Kenya.

The boys went home and disclosed the stranger's conversation with them to their parents. To the boys' surprise their parents were supportive. They encouraged Nicholas and George to spend more time on their studies in order to improve their chances of a successful professional career in their country. The boys agreed to abide by their parents rules and the following day after studying in the library they went to meet with the stranger at the address where he was coaching. The boys found a team comprising both older and younger men that were also very friendly. They had all the support they needed to thrive but almost became discouraged by the pressure of performance and the body aches from keeping fit. Soon, their bodies became used to the workouts. They continued to be with the team even after school summer break was over, they still trained in the evenings and during the weekends, as opposed to training seven hours daily a week as they'd done during the school breaks. The boys participated in local and national tournaments and by the time they were in the twelfth grade, they'd become star players in their positions and had earned many awards for themselves and their team.

When the twelfth grade national examination results were released, it was clear that the boys' hard work in school and with their basketball team had really paid off. Nicholas and George both attained grades that allowed them to study at any university of their choice in Kenya. However, they both decided to go beyond Kenya and applied to universities in Canada and the United States. These universities offered full scholarships for basketball talents the reason why these young men targeted such universities that had basketball teams that consistently achieved good results in the school champion leagues was to have a broader opportunity in pursing basketball. They were eventually accepted to different universities in Canada. Both schools were impressed with the boys' grades and with their previous performances on the basketball courts. Nicholas and George were offered full scholarship for their degree and masters programs because they played basketball for their institutions. George achieved a Masters of Arts in Sociology and

Nicholas Masters of Science in Mathematics. He is now teaching mathematics in the same institution and is also the head of sports department, where he continues to mentor young basketball players and also connects his school to local players in Kenya. George later moved back to Kenya and is now a director of a big non-governmental organization. He's also coaching the very team that coached him and Nicholas when they were teenagers. George serves as the main contact in Kenya when Nicholas requires new talented players for his university team in Canada. Nicholas and George's ability to accept doing something new has not only opened more doors for them and their families but also for other young and upcoming Kenyan basketball talents. It's crucial to have an open mind when considering trying new things. You never know where this may lead you, if not you, your community could benefit too

At this point and time in your life, the choice is all yours. Do you want to go ahead and reshape your destiny from here on or do you want it to fall apart?

Capable You –Everline Aboka   [26]

<u>This poem, entitled *You Chose* by Shannon L. Alder,</u> has helped me in a situation such as this.

You chose. You chose. You chose.

You chose to give away your love.
You chose to have a broken heart.
You chose to give up.
You chose to hang on.

You chose to react.
You chose to feel insecure.
You chose to feel anger.
You chose to fight back.
You chose to have hope.

You chose to be naïve.
You chose to ignore your intuition.
You chose to ignore advice.
You chose to look the other way.
You chose to not listen.
You chose to be stuck in the past.

Capable You –Everline Aboka   [27]

You chose your perspective.

You chose to blame.

You chose to be right.

You chose your pride.

You chose your games.

You chose your ego.

You chose your paranoia.

You chose to compete.

You chose your enemies.

You chose your consequences.

You chose. You chose. You chose. You chose.

However, you are not alone. Generations of women in your family have chosen. Women around the world have chosen. We all have chosen at one time in our lives. We stand behind you now screaming:

Choose to let go.

Choose dignity.

Choose to forgive yourself.

Choose to forgive others.

Choose to see your value.

Capable You –Everline Aboka   [28]

Choose to show the world you're not a victim.
Choose to make us proud.

Don't stay where you are now

Many of us may not be where we envision ourselves in life. We struggle and at times it seems as if we'll never be able to walk out of heartbreaking situations. The good news is that everybody in the world that's made it to the top in their particular field, has at some point dealt with struggles on their way to their glittering destiny.

Struggles is part of life, many times we don't have control over what happens or doesn't happen to us. Our attitude regarding what's going on around us at any given time is what defines whether we emerge as victors or victims, stronger or weaker, changed or destroyed, successful or unsuccessful. The reality is that life has to go on, no matter what you're facing. In 2003 when I was only a teenager, my father passed away. I felt as if I couldn't last for another day without him and all hope was lost for me at that point. Life seemed not only meaningless but also full of challenges. I could feel, and at times see, this in eyes of my mother and my siblings as we all struggled to cope. I can only imagine what my mother had to go through, raising seven children between the ages of three and nineteen all by herself. The love of her life that once stood six foot and seven inches tall was now resting six foot under. It was such a heart-wrenching situation. My siblings and I had to learn to deal with the fact that our father wasn't coming home ever again. Death had stolen the beautiful centerpiece of our home. He was too young to die yet he did.

From this experience I slowly changed from being daddy's little girl to mommy's responsible teenage girl. As my family's struggles continued after my father went to be with the Lord I had to drop out of school. My mother could no longer afford it and my eldest brothers didn't have a job to help out either. I decided to start plaiting people's hair at my mother's house. My three brothers Nick, Charles and Sunday carried luggage on their backs at the Kenya Ports Authority in Kisumu. Such form of employments brought in some money to buy food as our mother struggled at the other end with her small business to help pay for house utilities and of course rent, otherwise we'd have had no food, no school fees, no clothing, and worst of all no roof over our heads. Although I was busy plaiting hair and not going to school, my mind was still in class. I'd regularly caught up with my classmates, Susan Atieno Ochola and the late Caroline Adhiambo Ndar, to stay updated on what they were learning in school. I'd take notes from them, re-write them on my own books, and also make time in my busy days to study as often as I'd once done in my active school days. This went on for at least two years. I lost touch with teenage life, when my age mates were in school learning or attending events I was either plaiting hair or locked up in my room studying. I found myself in a new world, silence and focus became my friends and up to date, I still prefer to stay indoors and read a book than go out to a noisy and crowded place. Don't get me wrong, am not anti-social, in fact am the most charismatic lady you will ever meet. I just seem to prefer it quieter even though I can also be a party rock star in your party when situations calls for it.

Two years after episodes of struggle after dad's death, I decided to register for the twelfth grade final examination also known as the Kenyan Certificate of Secondary Education. Without attending eleventh and twelfth grade classes this was going to be a hard shot yet I got into it with confidence. It was a risk and it almost seemed like a joke to many. I was driven by the knowledge that I didn't want to stay where I was at that time. I wanted more. I believed that I was capable but for me to achieve anything beyond that point, I had to make a decision that I wasn't going to remain where I was, without a twelfth grade certificate. Either way, I had to move, making a leap of faith or something of that nature. Preparations for the examinations were not bread and butter and the ride was so bumpy that at times I felt like giving up. However I composed myself most of the time, studied as hard as I could and in October 2005 I faced the K.C.S.E examinations. When the results were available the following February, I realized that I hadn't attained the required university points to study law although my points did secure me a place in a professional college where I studied Journalism and Mass Communication. I achieved good grades, securing the points that gave me the chance to take a degree course in communications at the university in Canada many years later.

From this background that had once appeared to be so broken and hopeless God has enabled me to travel around the world as a fashion model. I've walked the runway in Canada, England, the United States, and in Africa. Life doesn't always give us what we want but we have to make a decision to live and even live better than we did before a tragedy hit. If life takes away your parent or loved one you need to make a decision to keep living. Live your life better so that your husband, child, parent, or whoever passed away would be very happy for you and proud that you did it, even in their absence.

I want to thank you so much for reading this book. The fact that you have it on your hands and that you've reached this line is an indication that you're on the road to making yourself a better person and that you're tired of where you currently are in life. I urge you not to stay where you are now. This is the first step toward change, knowing what you want and actually going for it. My wish is that this book will provide you with practical tips for your dream of moving on from your current situation to the place that you dream of in life.

Rise above your environment

We're all highly qualified to do even mightier things, although sometimes we may not realize this based on the environment in which we've constantly found ourselves. In most cases our environment tells us that we aren't capable, we can't do it, and that we aren't brilliant enough to accomplish our dreams. The good news is that you are qualified, says the Lord. When God created you He included all that you need to attain your destiny of greatness. Our environment includes not only our physical surroundings but also the spiritual, emotional, and social systems that we have around us. One of the greatest things I've learned is that not everyone is going to be for you, but that really doesn't matter. They don't have the same call and purpose you do for your dreams, only you have that. They don't have the visions for it, you do! So don't wait for their approval. I'm not advocating that you should be rude to people around you. My point is, if you realize that someone isn't helping you to be a better person, walk away from them in a nice way.

I was only sixteen when I felt deep in my heart that I wanted to model. One day I was reading a magazine featuring a spread about the then Miss Kenya on its pages. My neighbor, a friend's father, was seated next to me as I flipped through the magazine. I pointed to one of the photos and said ''one day, I'll be on this magazine as a model." To my surprise my friend's father told me that I'd never make it to that magazine. He informed me that I was a high school dropout and that models featured in the magazine were mainly university graduates from the country's most influential families. I knew that I didn't have such advantages. All I had was my dream and my precious family that seemed worthless to my neighbor. From that point I realized that for God to put that dream in me, He already knew me better. He was aware of my situation, how I would go about it and knew of the challenges that I would face along the way, including negativity from people that I encountered.

The man's words didn't break me but somehow stirred up something deeper about personal development. I decided not to break down nor engage in a battle of words with him. I couldn't even if I wanted to, he was old enough to be my father, my culture values respect and doing the opposite is not applauded. I shut my mouth, took my magazine to my room and wrote words of proclamation all over it. ''I will one day be featured in this magazine as a model.'' I then hung it on my wall. Soon every corner of my room was filled with photos of models, modelling shows and everything related to fashion. It was certainly true that most of the professional models belonged to the elite families of society but that didn't stop me from looking at those pictures every day and proclaiming that I too was going to be a successful model. It wasn't long before I'd plaited hair, saved enough money, registered for my high school certificate examinations, and sat for the national examinations.

A month after completing my final high school examinations, I learned of a local beauty pageant in my city yet was reluctant to participate. My peers that believed in my capability pushed me to the very day of the show to participate, they didn't care about the outcome even though they knew I would make it. All they wanted for me was to participate and for them to show me their support regardless of the outcome. You see, when this opportunity presented itself, a negative mentality was busy reminding of how bad I was, how I just came from the slums, or how my family wasn't making national headlines. For some reason I almost found myself buried under these lies and claims but thankfully God had also prepared peers who weren't going to allow me to miss participating in the show. I remember my friend Edmond K'Odero calling me in the afternoon a few hours before the show

''Triza, how come I don't see you here at the event venue? Everyone's here and the show will be on in a few hours." Said Edmond.

Fortunately that morning by the help of my mom's and my savings. I'd summoned enough courage to visit a salon only frequented by the elites and went into the city for hair dressing services. Upon hearing my phone conversation with Edmond the woman at the salon was very excited to hear that I was going to take part in a beauty pageant. She then offered to provide me with the best hair dressing services, more than I'd paid for, because she wanted people to know that she'd been a model's hair dresser. She even offered to accompany me to the show to do some touch ups to my hair after every change of looks at the show and above all to support me. With all that unexpected support around me, I walked that runway like a model in Milan, impressed the judges, the audience and was crowned Miss Tuungane 2005. This marked the beginning of the amazing journey of my modelling career. Yet the challenges didn't stop there. When I finally signed up with an agency in Nairobi and began going to various auditions to book jobs, I faced even bigger, heart wrenching rejections, such as being informed that I was too skinny, too tall, too dark, or too softly spoken but none of these stopped me. I pushed and rose above these environments that were screaming mediocrity and failure and walked out with victory on my side. When I reached the international modelling level, I was accepted unopposed. Everybody wanted and always wants to work with me as a model. Such situations are said to strengthen us, but most of the time we dwell too much on what the environment is feeding us and forget that we can also create our own powerful environments in our brains. These self-created environments can oppose all the negative comments generated by the outside environment. I challenge you to create your own powerful environment that mainly speaks of success, favor, victory, and blessings, along with all the other positive words that you would love to feature in your life. Maybe you were once told that you'd never make it in life? Those words probably stung so deep that many years later you can still feel their impact. I strongly suggest that you attempt to rise above that environment of failure and speak words of success over your life. You could declare that you're going to lead a successful and prosperous life from today and remind yourself of this whenever you encounter a situation where you feel that you only have a slim chance of success.

You may come from a dysfunctional family or live in the slums. You might feel that there is no hope in life, but I know people that are currently part of a wonderful family, even though they experienced a rough childhood in which their parents divorced or separated. I was born and raised in the slums but I don't live there anymore, I hope that gives you hope that you are not meant to die where you are now. I had hopes of living in North America and today I live in Canada, after years of not thinking and acting like a lady from Nyalenda. I lived in the slums but I had bigger visions beyond the slums. Every struggle in that slum did not end up being a stumbling block but a stepping stone to my dreams.

When you have a dream and a vision this doesn't mean that you'll have a smooth ride devoid of obstacles. It's up to you to decide to rise above the challenges you'll encounter. Before Moses was chosen to lead the Israelites to the promised land Moses knew that he stammered but that didn't change God's plan. He'd already defined Moses' destiny for him and the same thing applies to us. All we need to do is to believe that we can do it, without complaints or excuses, just getting out there and doing it. The dream living within you is not a coincidence and you being chosen for it is not a mistake. Keep pushing that door and if it doesn't open as you push it gently, go ahead and break it down, after all we have all never had of someone who died from finding his way into a presented opportunity. From what I know, it is the nature of an opportunity to only knock on the door but doesn't break it. If your name isn't Mr. or Mrs. Opportunity, I challenge you to stop being gentle, break down that door, and fight for your rightful destiny. By now you know your talents. You need to decide what you can do to turn them into something beautiful, into something successful that you're pleased to spend time on.

Chapter 2
That Daring You

In this chapter we'll explore just about everything that will help us to find our way to planning our dreams and goals, the challenges that we're likely to encounter in our pursuit of success and the small but very important details that we can't do without when it comes realizing our dreams. All you need to do at the end of the day is to dare to dream about success and the things that you want to see happen in your life.

Plan to successfully use your gifts

"Planning is bringing the future into the present so that you can do something about it now."
Alan Lakein

It's only by planning that we can visualize the future of something even before it begins. Without planning, we may not know where we want to go or even where to start. Without planning we become blind to even the simplest steps. Human brains are the hub of a great metropolitan city. Our minds are always building or breaking down castles, processing or dispersing information. It's so busy inside our brains that we can't even imagine that we can keep everything in there and run smoothly without the reminders derived from well written plans

I recently decided to investigate the housing market in my city. I knew exactly what I wanted so when I met with the realtor I was very specific regarding the style, the appliances and the overall interior and exterior finish of the house. I needed a house that was newly built but still incorporated some exterior colonial era designs. My realtor conducted a thorough search and located a house that I loved so much. The design was much better than what I was looking for, the floor plan suited my style, the finishing and appliances were very modern and upgraded, just the way I wanted them. I really wanted to meet the contractor that had built the house and if possible to meet the architect too. The realtor was very supportive and managed to connect me with the contractor. When we sat down to talk about the house the contactor told me that his secret was to deliver far and beyond expectations. In this way all the houses he has built, turned out perfectly and his clients are never disappointed.

Focus on the vision

The contractor explained that the architect needed to be aware not only of the contractor's plans but also the client's requirements. This helped them to perfectly put together an exact picture in the form of a house plan to act as a step-by-step guide for everyone from the foundation to the completion of the house's construction. It's interesting to note that without the plan, there's no house. Similarly, we won't have success in using our gifts if we don't have a plan to realize our vision and to guide our steps on a daily basis toward our primary goal. The contractors bring together the materials, tools and workers to create the final product but the house plan becomes a contractor's best friend so that at every stage they consult the plan. Nothing can be changed after the construction process has started. If there are any modifications these should be made before the plan is approved and it doesn't matter how significant the change might be. Any mistake in construction is dealt with as soon as it arises otherwise the contractor risks having to tear down the whole building down. A tiny mistake can affect the entire house because the construction work isn't completed according to the plan's specifications.

By now you must have realized the importance of a vision for your dreams in your planning process. Perhaps the simplest illustration would be the approach I adopted when I decided to start modelling. My vision and mission was to share the love of God with people who worked in the fashion industry. My goal accompanying that vision was to simply strut the fashion runway not only in Kenya but also all over Africa, and in Canada, London, and in the fashion capitals of Europe. Committing this to paper played a big role in my modelling career and today I've achieved this goal and vision. I'm still moving forward, glory be to God almighty, the maker of all things beautiful including myself. The amazing power that watch over me in this race and redirect me whenever challenges threaten me with words of defeat. Today I challenge you to dare to dream big and have a goal, vision, and mission.

Create powerful daily declarations/ affirmations
I've realized that we're all who we are today in part because of the words we speak about ourselves. Our tongues are so powerful that we can create an amazing life for ourselves or simply waste it by how we use our tongue. Our minds, souls, and mouths are always working together, in line with what our destiny holds for us. Words coming out of mouth are like seeds. They not only grow but also flourish and bear fruit. If what we speak about our children, our family, our work, our talents, our spouses, or ourselves grow and bear fruits, so why don't we plant powerful words in our lives, their lives and situations?

When I was growing up we knew a young lady that was brilliant but like me her father passed away when she was only teenager. Her uncle had a job and was able and willing to pay her high school fees. She was always the best in her class but by grade ten I realized a tagline in all her books. This tagline that read ''born to suffer'' appeared right beneath the name, class, and subject. From my experience in Kenyan high school, I know that most students become hard to work with by grade ten. They become stubborn both in school and at home. They get involved with dangerous groups and only listen to their peers, who are as high as they are. This was the case for this young lady as well. She was young, only in grade ten and was struggling to find her purpose in life. She believed that she was a tough lady and that if anybody was going to punish her for her actions they'd need to know in advance that she didn't care because she was ''born to suffer''. It only took a year for the words of this young girl to begin affecting her life. She quit school, got involved with the bad groups around her neighborhood, and ran away from home for more than two years. When she finally decided to return, she met an irresponsible man and became pregnant. To make matters worse, the pressure of her relationship with this man resulted in her having a miscarriage. She didn't have a chance to carry her own baby. As a young woman I felt her pain but I didn't know how to help her. Many years later I realized that this brilliant young girl had predicted her future with the words she constantly used. Even though she wasn't attending school and not using her books with the destructive ''born to suffer'' tagline, many years later the fruits from the seeds of those words became a reality in her life.

Words, whether used recklessly or carefully, or with good, bad or no intent, can still manifest themselves into our lives. I'm considered to be a very positive person. I tend to encourage myself and people around me. I've learnt that negative things happen in life, ''so what?'' we have no option but to stay positive in all situations because the moment we let misery take charge we're headed for complete destruction. For us to realize success, we need our words and actions to be in line with the success that we're aiming for. We can't expect to be healthy when we keep telling people how sick we are. Even though I don't expect you to lie about your health, I still believe it's powerful to say, ''I'm getting better,'' even if healing is yet to appear. The words, ''I'm getting better,'' will allow your brain to send information of ''getting better / feeling better'' to the body's aching parts. The message will be, ''hello, wake up, and get better,'' as opposed to when you use words that mean the opposite. For example, saying ''I'm still sick,'' will make you feel even worse because ''am sick'' is all that's been deposited in your brain. Consequently this sends that sickness signal to your body, which will have no option but to feel as directed.

If you're dreaming of a life that is full of health, wealth, abundance, wisdom, inspiration, influence, favor, possibilities, and prosperity, it's important that you declare that those things are part of your life right now, even if you seem so far away from your vision. If possible, write your life the way you want to see it or how you visualize it, take a few minutes to say those words out loud on a daily basis and work your way towards those words. At the end of the day it's the words and the actions. There are many daily affirmations/ declarations to choose from but if you're uncertain how to get started rest assured that it's an easy task. First and foremost, when writing your declarations you need to make sure that they're positive. "I am blessed'' portrays an event as it has already happened, so use ''blessed'' and avoid the use of future tense such as ''I will be blessed.'' That should be easy and breezy, right?

An example of a daily declaration/affirmation
I am blessed, I am healthy, I am strong, I am intelligent, I am kind, I am loving and I am a wonderful person. I have a good personality, I am rich, I am prosperous, I am successful, I am a child of the most high God, I am an overcomer, I am honorable, I am compassionate, I am honest, I am anointed of the Lord, I am the apple of God's eye, I am the most loved of the Lord, I am creative, I am victorious. God has me in the palm of his hands. I am an overcomer, I am blessed coming in and going out. God is turning my life around for victory. God is watching over me.

I am fun to be around, people are drawn to me. I am an engaging person, I am beautiful I am attractive, I am equipped, I am approved, I am set apart for greatness, and I am destined to live in abundance. God is renewing my strength. I fly high like an eagle. I am excited about this beautiful day and I am more than a conqueror. I excel in everything I do, I am a quick learner, I have excellent study habits, I am a good listener and I am full of knowledge, wisdom and understanding. I believe the best in people as I do to me. I am blessed by everyone who I shall meet today. I am connected to the right people. I am a blessing to many, the light of God radiates all round my life. I am strong in the Lord. I can do all things through Christ who strengthens me. I am well able to fulfill my destiny, am a better person by each passing day, and made perfectly.

I am blessed to have a caring mother. She is healthy, strong, wise, kind, loving, blessed, wonderful, successful, God loving, favored, and she has unquestionable knowledge and understanding. My brothers, sisters, husband, children, grandchildren, nephews, nieces, are blessed, heathy, favored, strong, intelligent, blessed, rich, kind, loving, prosperous, successful, and God loving. You can create a daily declaration that speaks to each and every aspect of your life, your parents, spouse, brothers, sisters, nephews, nieces and any other person that you feel you're so connected to that you'd love to see their lives shine. Everywhere I have been and every influential person I have met or admire tells me that they've realized the success in their lives and much of the outcome is based on how they have channeled and still channel their words to their thoughts and work. Working hard with a negative attitude only gives birth to more and more negativity and negative outcomes.

How to get the best out of your daily declarations
Its one thing to write daily declarations but quite another to use them with knowledge to achieve that desirable change you want in your life. I consider myself to be reasonably tech-savvy but I'm also old school. I'll show up at meetings with a notebook, a laptop, and an iPad but still prefer to write on my

notebook. The feeling is completely different from typing electronically and much easier to use for reference. Write your daily affirmations on a paper, a note book or a journal. Something physical like a pen and a paper makes a whole lot difference than typed or recorded affirmations.

After writing them down. Find a time when you can completely switch off from everything and declare or say these words out. You don't have to shout but remember you should say them with a voice of power, confidence and assurance. Make your body and mind believe in those words you are declaring, because it is the belief that your entire body has in those declarations that will make them come to pass. Practice this often and have the words with you everywhere you go so that if you happen to meet any obstacles in form of discouragements at any time of the day, you can then pull them out and your declarations and recite them again. If you are prayerful, you can as well include these in your prayer time.

Grow from your failures, learn from mistakes

We tend to fill our minds with delusional expectations when we begin pursuing anything in life. The biggest mistakes that we make are in believing that we can't fail and that we know what we're doing very well. We should instead acknowledge that we're embarking on an adventurous journey and plan to go with the flow, learn from every challenge that comes with it and grow from these challenges. We all come from households where success is celebrated while failure is frowned upon and sometimes cruelly punished. Our society fails to understand that not all success happens instantly. Behind every successful man or woman lies a long trail of failure, disappointments, and challenges but most importantly it's our determination, perseverance, and tenacity we have acquired through our failures, challenges and disappointments that pull us through the other side of success.

It's okay to fail. Yes, you can read that again. I said that it's okay to fail as long as you are brave enough to turn that failing moment into a learning experience. In most cases, these failures push us to want even more. Without failure the road to success is a relatively peaceful yet boring adventure that nobody would want to be part of, except for the faint at heart that will never inherit the kingdom of success anyways. Imagine any innovation that that leaves you astonished and consider the inventors. Do you think we'd have such amazing end products if the inventors didn't encounter obstacles along the way and worked to overcome them? If they'd simply given up we'd have products that only match the mediocrity of the non-challenging environment present during the innovation stages.

The Apple products that we all enjoy using today didn't just happen. People put so much effort into making them happen. Think of the late Steve Jobs and his founding of Apple, his journey while developing the products we have today, and the moments when he must have felt as if the whole world was against his products and his company. His perseverance, tenacity, and higher ambitions prepared him to deliver far and beyond products that we enjoy using today such as MacBook, iPads, iPhones, iPods, I Watches and so many other Apple products.

Create a message from that mess

"Successful people maintain a positive focus in life no matter what is going on around them. They stay focused on their past successes rather than their past failures, and on the next action steps they need to take to get them closer to the fulfillment of their goals rather than all the other distractions that life presents to them"
Jack Canfield

I heard of about a fashion model that worked as a prostitute most of her life. She went to church one day feeling as if her entire life was over and everything was crumbling on her feet. She wanted a new encounter, a new direction, and a new foundation to her life. She'd lived a miserable life and was ready to start all over again. She entered the church and the usher directed her to the front row where she sat patiently, listening carefully and with the desire to meet God that might transform her life. As soon as the altar call was made, the woman walked to the pulpit and before the pastor led her in prayers, she knelt down and cried.

"'Lord, God, if for sure you exist, come and save me and transform my life.''
This woman encountered a new beginning and little by little found herself not going to work as a prostitute in the evenings any more. She went to church often, mingled with the right people, who led her to knowledge and encouraged her that she was doing the right thing. She decided to invest her savings from her prostitution job in a small catering business in her town, supplying food for corporate events, parties, and funerals. Before long she was an employer of other prostitutes from her previous job, with whom she also helped to transform their lives.

She later established a community organization that traveled around her city and country, encouraging prostitutes to come out, share their pain, and find emotional, financial and psychological help to better their lives and the lives of their children. Whenever I think about this woman, I can't fathom the humiliation she went through, sharing her pain with people that may or may not have understood her pain because they didn't experience it firsthand. Did she fear that some would judge her? The only outstanding virtue about this woman was her desire to change after realizing that she'd messed up. The moment we realize that we're a bunch of messed up individuals it becomes so easy for us to accept that we need help. What follows is finding that help, getting renewed, and living the life that is part of our planned destiny.

As you read this book, I must say that I don't have any idea of the mess that you're in but I know that I don't want your story to end where you are now. You are a child of the highest God, approved by God Himself, blessed, and with God's help you're capable of being highly successful in your life. Don't sit there feeling sorry for yourself. Don't be sad. You're not the first person to be in such a mess and if this will make you cheer up, let me remind you that you're not going to be the last person to be in such a mess either.

Move ahead and give way to other upcoming beautiful events in your life. In this way you'll be able to help those in the same situation in the future after you've accepted the need to move forward and get ushered into your planned destiny. Whatever is that is keeping you from moving, if you keep giving it room in your life, feeding it in your thoughts, and clothing it inside your brain, it will prevent you from reaching your destiny. The moment that you will decide you don't need that monster dragging you down, that's the moment you'll move on to greater levels that you never thought you'd experience.

Stay focused, stay optimistic, stay hopeful. Be on the move because we can't achieve that which lies in our future if we constantly spend more time going back to pick up the many broken pieces of our past lives. Anything broken is cumbersome to carry. That messed up past life is heavy and awkward to carry in your heart and mind. Let it go and focus on tomorrow. Your destiny will thank you for it.

Clear your mind of that victim mentality and start declaring that you're a victor. You possess the key to all that happens in your life. This key was rightfully given to you at the moment that you were born. Many people mistakenly believe that they don't own this key and that it's only in the hands of your parents, teachers, spouses, church leaders, or some other person in authority but this is completely false. You have the key in your hands. Use it wisely to unlock your full potential because all that you need is already yours. Rise up from your troubles and create an inspiring message that many others can learn from. The time for belly dancing, complaining and being complacent is over, arise, shine and fly with the eagles. Don't remain in the level of the caterpillar, go past that stage of crawling and simply spread your wings and fly away. I can assure that when you start to fly above the skies, you will have a better vision of this life. My friend, you are an eagle, stop hanging around chickens or situations that bring you down. Have an eagle mentality of soaring above the clouds and soar above your obstacles, disappointments and challenges in life. ''Oh yes you can do this. You are capable, go for it my beloved reader''

Stay focused on your goals

So many people fail to realize their potential because they have no goal at all. They're just doing things just for the sake of them, to pass the time, or because their parents or teachers want them to do those things. A goal is the object of a person's ambition or effort, an aim or desired result. We have to truly identify the result we desire based on the simple things that we do that also consume our time. We can't invest in anything and expect to get nothing from it. Our actions will result in either good or bad results even especially if we don't make our goals clear. However, bad results always land us in trouble, either with our parents, spouses, family, friends, law enforcement, or even the school system. This does seem to result in wasted time when we want to correct the mistakes that steal the time we'd have invested in transforming ourselves into those better people that we wish to be.

If you go to school, don't just wake up then arrive in class without knowing what you expect from that day. Good study habits begin with knowing your class timetable or routine on a weekly basis and planning ahead by studying ahead too. The same applies to our future dreams, ambitions, and talents. We need to have goals because they help us to run everything smoothly. Let's look at how we can stay focused to successfully achieve our dreams.

Write clear goals with timeline
Most successful people will tell you that the reason they have written goals is because their lives gets busier and from busy life, chaos are inevitable. Learn to set your goals, weather simple or complex, write them down and have a time frame you desire to achieve them.

As I mentioned earlier, our brains are a busy hub, more hectic than the New York stock exchange. Our brains are constantly working. We're constantly thinking and taming our mind becomes easier only when we start to write down our goals. We can achieve a great deal with a tamed mind. It always feels good to be in control of what we do so why can't we take control of our own minds? Taming your mind is a clear indication that you're becoming a better person. You are headed for success. Why not give it a try by setting your goals and working to achieve them?

I know that devising clear goals can be a daunting task to already busy individual, but such goals are essential if we want to reach our highest potential. Goal writing is something we need to do, whether we want to or not. Not writing down our goals only leads us astray, leaving us confused and unfocused. For goals to be achievable they must also be as simple as possible. So please slow down, breathe in and grab your pen and paper so that you can do it.

Let's look at few steps related to how to write clear goals.

Write goals about the things you love, desire, or dream about

It would be pointless for us to write goals that aren't born from within us. You can't let the desires of your parents, teachers, spiritual leaders, children, friends, or relatives or even an author like myself became your own desires. It never works that way because we're unique individuals with unique talents and gifts so our dreams and desires can't all be identical. Even if you have a twin, or someone you share close similarities, your dreams, desires, and wants will still differ from each other. This shouldn't scare you but rather make you feel good about yourself and the capabilities that you possess to create a direction in your life. Even though the individuals in your circle can help you in terms of encouragement and being there for you through your daunting task of writing your goals, it's not advisable that they impose their own personal goals on you. Sometimes what others want for us may sound ideal, but this doesn't mean that it'll be good for us in the long run.

If you're in your final year at high school, you love mathematics and you desire to pursue a career in it, it's important you write your goal. For example:

- *Start part-time accounting job at the university cafeteria*
- *Graduate with Bachelor of Science in mathematics after four years*
- *Teach mathematics at your university or another local college*

You'll realize that no matter how big or small the dream, we remained in the areas that incorporated mathematics. When we direct our goals to reflect the desires and dreams we have about life, the load of boredom, discouragement, and defeat is naturally lifted up from our shoulders. We smoothly sail to our dream's destination and should we encounter a storm, our zeal is far greater than the tribulation.

Write detailed goals

I happen to be someone who loves details. They not only make things run smoothly but also save us time and energy. Creating detailed goals is just as important as creating the goals in the first place. Imagine you're a young couple just starting your lives after marriage. The woman is already two months pregnant and you're faced with a decision to buy a house at least two months before your first baby arrives. You've agreed that you need a house that has a master bedroom, two bedrooms for your future children, a spare bedroom for when your parents are visiting, at least two full bathroom suites, a modern kitchen, a garage, a man's cave for the man of the house, and a play area for the children, all with a budget of $500,000. A detailed goal for this case might look something like this:

- *Contact a realtor, find and buy a home with four bedrooms, play area, modern kitchen, large living space, extra room and a garage, worth $500,000 dollars in 5 months' time.*

- *Search home listings online and buy a home with four bedrooms, play area, modern kitchen, large living space, extra room and a*

*garage, worth $500,000 dollars in 5 months'
time.*

Whether you choose to hire a realtor or decide to hunt
for a home yourselves, you'd still stick to the goal of
getting the house with the specifications you want
and within your designated time frame.

Match your goals

I'm sure there's always someone, somewhere, who
has his or her goals all mixed up, gets confused in the
event, and ends up with nothing in the long run. We
can all avoid this dilemma by making sure that our
dreams aren't contradicting each other in our life.
Chaos and confusion usually end in failure and we
don't want that to happen to us. Therefore we must
know how to match our goals all the time. A good
example would be a youth raised in the church, who
wishes to be a pastor one day. Ideally, you'd expect
this young man to spend much of his time studying
the bible and avoiding any other books that contradict
the teachings of Christianity. The moment this young
man starts to study other books about different

religions he'll notice confusion in the teachings and might even abandon his goal of pastoring a church. Of course if this man wants to later teach people about the differences between various beliefs then his approach to studying more than one religion will be to his advantage.

Another example of a way to match your dreams could be derived from someone who loves to write and address the public with informational material. Perhaps someone that also wants to publish a book on self-awareness and simultaneously distribute audio messages about the same book before the end of 2015. This person could have these two goals well catered for in her life simply because writing and public speaking fall into the category of communication. As a writer, I'm able to convert my written message into audio messages or I can convert my audio messages into written work, which works pretty well. A few examples of such a goal would be:

- *Publish a self-awareness book from the same audio message by November 2015*

- *Record audio message on a self-awareness book and distribute online by November 2015*

You'll notice that these two goals will be easier to accomplish for this person because either way, one of the goals will eventually lead to another. It doesn't matter which one he or she starts with, both goals will eventually be achieved because they match one another.

Write positive goals

Since the day I learnt the power of all the words we speak throughout our lives, I've become addicted to positivity, everywhere I go. Even if people are in mourning I tend to see the brighter side of that situation than the depressing part of it. If positivity affects our lives a big deal then why eliminate it from the most important step in life, the writing of the goals of our lives? It all comes down to the power of our subconscious mind. This is almost like our checking account at the bank. If we deposit ten dollars in our checking account this will be reflected in our account balance. If we deposit one million dollars that's also going to show up in your account balance. Because we occasionally revisit our goals on a daily or weekly basis to determine if we are still on track, it's important that the words of those goals reflect exactly what we want and the way in which we want to see it happen. Our subconscious mind identifies yes as yes, no as no, and maybe as maybe. I know that on occasion people say these words and their face expresses the opposite and your subconscious mind can read that too.

For example, if you've worked hard, earned your money, and your dream is to own a $5 million mansion with a private pool in Florida by December 2015. Your goal should read like this:

- *Buy a mansion with a private pool in Florida at the cost of $5 million by December 2015*

But not like this:

- *Maybe buy a mansion with private pool at the cost of $5 million by December 2015*

Based on both examples above, buying a home will surely happen in the first case but in the second case the chances are slim that either buying or not buying will take place. It doesn't matter how much we push towards our dreams in life. If we have the maybe or no mentality we can never realize our greatest potential. *The favors, blessings, and elevations of the Lord end in yes and amen. Nothing more, nothing less.* The picture of the life we desire is first developed in our minds through our thoughts, dreams, and desires. Yet the reality of living that life depends on us having positive thoughts and believing in the possibility of all these happening to us regardless of our family background, status in society, or level of education. We have the ability to attract success, wealth, fame, and prosperity on the contrary we also have the ability to attract the opposite.

When I wake up in the morning, I go to the bathroom or closet mirror, smile at myself and tell myself, "Good morning, you beautiful lady? Today you look even more beautiful than those other days!'' I then follow up with powerful declarations like I am blessed, I am healthy, I am prosperous, I am redeemed by the blood of the Lord, I am highly favored, I am the apple of His eyes, and my cup overflows. I am a lender, I am an overcomer, I am destined for greatness and my light shines bright. I am strong, I am listener, I radiate with joy, am at peace, my mind is alert, I am intelligent and I am kind. I continue to declare the same powerful words on behalf of my mother, my husband, my brothers and sisters, my nephews and nieces, as well as my unborn children. I've become such a friend of positive talking and thinking that my friends and peers think I either have no feelings or am just ignoring life situations. The reality is if life has happened and I have no power to change it at least I can change how my mind will react to that life situation. Yes, I can change how I think about the whole situation. If I have negative thoughts I'll end up being stressed as a result the trouble will be doubled, combining the stress of my misfortune and the stress I inflict on myself by thinking negatively about something that I can't change? I lose nothing by thinking positively in a situation I cannot change. However, I invite the spirit of joy that gives way to a peaceful mind, which in return leads to faster healing process from the recent misfortune.

To give you hope, know that I have written this book at a time when life has taken me to another curve and I was going through one of the toughest moments in my life since I moved to Canada in 2012. You may wonder why I would be writing a book when going through a tough time. I realized that I had more quiet times than I did many years ago and decided to turn this whole situation into something positive. Instead of lying down on the bed, feeling bad about everything and crying as if the whole world was crumbling around me, I decided to write this book. Throughout this process I have found peace, courage, and stamina to not only talk to you but to offer encouragement to you too during the tough moments in your life. Every night I would struggle to fall asleep, so I would reach out for a glass of warm water, pick up my laptop and my notebook and continue to write. With family far away in Kenya and

I missing them dearly, especially my mother, loneliness, sorrow and heartache could easily take root but I choose to make friends with my laptop in the wee hours when sleep is out of reach.

Go far and beyond what you can accomplish

When setting our goals, we tend to confuse simple and precise for small and mediocre. A dream can still be simple, clear, and yet still ambiguous and achievable at the same time. The goal's ambiguity is determined by the effect it will have on your life and that of others, upon its realization.

When I began my modelling career I started at the community level. After that all my other goals on the same dream had to go a notch higher. If not I wouldn't be making any progress but just marking time in the same place if I choose not to reach for the oranges on the tallest branch of the tree. We all know that given time oranges on the lowest part of the tree fall to the ground and begin to rot. It's the same with our achievements. They eventually lose value, calling on us to go further and beyond what we've accomplished today.

Going far and beyond gives you the excitement of trying something you've never attempted before. It increases your zeal and stamina to expand your knowledge in an area of expertise or with a talent that you've been developing. For example, perhaps you've been playing basketball for your school team and at the completion of twelfth grade you still plan to play but don't know which team to join. In this case you might consider joining a basketball team at the university or playing for a local community or corporation. Going back to play for your high school team might not give you the more experience you need. In most cases you'll find that you will gain much experience playing for your university, in your community, or even for a small corporation at the county league level. When faced with writing a goal for this type of situation you could write as follows:

- *Join the university basketball team, play for them for four years and win awards every year*

- *Join the community basketball team, represent them for four years from county to nationwide league and win awards every year*
- *Join a company basketball team, represent them in corporate leagues for four years and win awards every year*

Such goals take you further ahead and don't mean that you need to compete again for awards that you've already won. My transition was simple from community as Miss Tuungane, to district, as Miss International Women's Day Kisumu, and to provincial level as Miss Wakilisha Na Trust Kenya. I then moved on to nationwide as a Miss World Kenya finalist, to Africa as an M-Net Face of Africa finalist, to North America as African- Canadian Model of the year, and finally worldwide as the Top Model worldwide winner. If we have such arrangements in our goals and dreams, we not only grow but also give others room to grow. For example, in 2015 I declined a straight nomination for Canadian model of the year simply because I wanted other young and upcoming models to have an opportunity to grow and let their work be known in the industry as well. I feel good when other people grow, that's just the way I am. I know it's a rare quality in the competitive modeling industry but I know that I'm not called to be like everyone else but to stand out in my character and my professional ethics. Now let's examine the second way to successfully stay focused on your goals.

Have a daily to do list

These kinds of lists are common. They can be kept in tiny notebooks or you can use the power of technology to plan daily goals without missing an activity. With the use of technology you can plan every aspect of your daily routines by simply synching phone contacts to emails, to do lists, and to your alarm. For example, if you have to practice your vocals at four o'clock every afternoon your phone can notify in advance about this event, where it's taking place, how long it will take you to get to the venue by car, walking or transit, the list of people joining you for this event and how long the event will last. If you find technology too complicated, you can still write your to do lists manually by highlighting the activity, the people involved, venue, time and then you might need to inform the people that will accompany you. I tend to write my to do lists when an activity comes to mind or an appointment shows up. There's no recommended day of the week or month to add information to a list, except for the time an activity comes to mind. If your vocal practices are scheduled daily at four o'clock in the afternoon, each week and each month, then such an event can be planned for monthly and should be marked appropriately on your calendars so that you don't miss it by including another activity in its place. The road to success demands the creation of a strict timetable. This must be followed to the letter without compromise, unless somebody is dying and your attention is needed to save their life, then yes, you are allowed not to follow the timetable.

Follow up with your goals to the later
It's easy to write goals. Following them to the latter is another story and requires competency and self-discipline. People can teach you how to follow up with your goals but you alone are responsible for

making sure that these goals are followed to the point of accomplishment.

The one motivation that can help us follow through with our goals is by engaging our imagination. Picture how it might feel to finally achieve that goal and eliminate anything that might be a distraction. If your goal is to lose 10kg from your current weight, your reasons for losing that weight could be to become healthier, keep fit, to fit into fashionable clothes that you see in stores in the mall, or just generally to make you feel good about yourself. While attempting to achieve a goal involving weight loss, you're likely to stumble upon obstacles such as deep fried donuts, French fries, and similar fatty foods that you know that you should avoid when you're trying to keep fit and lose weight. It's up to you as an individual to instill self-discipline into your routine to enable you to fight food cravings and temptations when trying to shed those pounds.

Another secret is be respectful of your goals. It's funny that we really expect people to respect our goals while our goals really wish that we give them a bit of the same respect before we move outwards to look for the same. Respect to your goals starts with you. It's more of an inside job before you take it outwards. People are likely to see your commitments to your goals and appreciate you for it but only when you are truly committed to your goals with actions not just saying it.

Rewrite clearer goals

So you've already written all your goals clearly, made a daily to do list, followed up with your dreams until you've accomplished them, or the time frame you set has expired but you didn't accomplish your dreams yet. What do you do now? Do you give up? No, it's not time to give up yet. In fact there is never a time to give up. You got to push through till you come out with your desired extraordinary results. We all face similar situations involving unaccomplished goals. Yet giving up at this stage will only prove to you that you're incompetent, disrespectful, and untrustworthy. You need to go back to the drawing board and rewrite all your goals.

Often we either experience great joy if we're able to achieve our dreams or too much pain when we miss our target. At this stage you need to become your own number one fan. It doesn't matter whether you won or lost. You have an opportunity at this stage to look at yourself in the mirror and tell yourself, "Good job, you beautiful lady/handsome man. I'm very proud of you that you managed to follow up with your goals this far. We may have missed a few points but we can make it next time.'' There's nothing as powerful and encouraging as speaking to oneself. That's my hobby and I can tell you that am not crazy, I am one hundred percent normal. I encourage myself in front of my mirrors and I love it. I do it to the point that I'm laughing with myself. It feels good because at the end of the day you still manage to give yourself what the world did not offer you at that time. Why wait for an encouragement from someone else who might never give it to you while you can actually encourage yourself? People won't applaud you all the time so you have to learn to applaud yourself even in the midst of a mess. We all know that people can also sometimes decide to put us down, even in obvious times when we have performed excellently, this hurts us to the point where we feel that all our self-esteem and confidence has been thoroughly crushed on. Why wait for them to inflict negativity on you when you can boost your own morale by feeding yourself a lot of positivity?

The enemy knows as soon that as they feed you negativity you become discouraged, have low self-esteem, become afraid, and wouldn't want to meet anyone, let alone go out and try again. This is the enemy's greatest tool that he uses to deter us from reaching our highest potential. He reminds us that we failed and that we'll surely fail again if we try, which is totally false. Always remember that you have the keys to anything that happens to your life. You can use your key of positivity to put the enemy down and work toward achieving your goals once again.

Once you've dealt with the feelings of disappointment about not achieving your goals, you'll have to go back to the drawing board. Follow the steps we've already covered to attain clear goals in the future and write new goals that will enable you to achieve even more. This is the point where you think bigger again, as you grow, let your goals grow too.

If you failed to achieve your goals it's important that you perform a review and determine the reasons that you feel hindered you. Make a commitment that the same hindrances will not take a toll on you again and start by rewriting these goals before you move ahead to new ones. Once you're convinced regarding your potential outcomes, you can then move to other goals.

Keep your destiny connectors close

Destiny connectors are those people that make you long to do more in order to realize your life's dreams. There are two types of destiny connectors.

Positive destiny connectors

Positive destiny connectors are the ones that you should keep closest to you. These are the people that support you regardless of a situation to ensure that you achieve your dreams to the fullest. Positive destiny connectors can be your parents, siblings, friends, teachers, co-workers, spouse, fans or many other individuals. These are the people that you'll constantly hear reminding you that they're very proud of you, even for the smallest accomplishments. They're always present to offer you all kinds of help including spiritual, financial, material and emotional support. Positive destiny connectors are strategically placed in your life so that they can focus on supporting you. This reminds you that when God brings an opportunity He not only creates a way to that opportunity but a means to reach it too. Your positive destiny connectors could be your means to your destiny.

"A mother's love for her child is like nothing else in the world. It knows no awe, no pity, it dares all things and crushes down remorselessly all that stands in its path."
Agatha Christie

Throughout my life I've been so lucky to have these people who carry me on their shoulders to help me realize my potential. One of them is my mother, Anna

Awour Aboka, a woman of character and virtue. I've literally watched this precious woman raise seven children single-handedly, conducting a little business here and there to make ends meet. My mother loves her children so much that she'd rather have us all eat the food while she goes without. I've developed so much respect for my mother. Having travelled all around the world, I must admit that I haven't met a selfless woman like my mother. She tops the list of all my destiny connectors because she has always been there for me. Five months after my conception, my mom faced a severe uterine bleeding problem that threatened my survival as a fetus as well as hers. She was at home with my four elder brothers in umala village of Alego Siaya. As a young woman in her mid-twenties my mother had seen the signs of a miscarriage earlier that morning but thought it was just minor spotting that would clear up during the day. Unfortunately the spotting turned into severe bleeding that night since she'd been busy during the day with household chores. What else could she do at home alone and with four children to take care of? At around ten at night that day, my mom asked my elder brother, who hadn't even celebrated his tenth birthday yet, to go to my mother's aunt and inform her that, ''mommy was very sick and needed help." By the time my mom's aunt Jennifer, her husband, the late Oganga K'Ogada, and my uncle Vincent arrived, my mother had collapsed and had to be rushed to the hospital. Upon her arrival the doctors had slim hopes that my mother would able to pull through and respond positively to the treatments. She had lost a lot of blood and her skin color changed from brown to yellow. It did seemed as if she might would not make but my mother's a strong woman, she got through her painful experience. Seven days later she left the hospital after the doctors had confirmed that both she and I were fine.

Two months later my mother was in the same hospital bed, fighting for her life and mine once again after she realized that she was having another case of uterine bleeding. Why am I sharing so much about this story? Well, I realize that my life and accomplishments wouldn't be possible without my mother's fight for life. Without that I wouldn't be here today. My mother gave me life and in the process she almost lost hers. She battled two uterine bleeding that were no doubt leading to miscarriages. She fought a good fight, defeated the enemy, and pushed me out into existence. The most amazing part about my birth is that when I was born, I weighed 4.1kg. Many thought I would be tiny and end up in the nursery room but I was born through normal delivery at 6 o'clock in the morning. At ten o'clock in the morning on the following day my mother took me home. My mother Anna has not only been there for me in my childhood. She's still here for me today. She's attended as many of my contests as possible, she prays for me, encourages me, and reminds me that I'm highly favored and blessed to excel beyond what I can imagine. My mother never sees any difficulty in anything. If you're seeking something she'll tell you in a calm voice, ''just keep calm, you shall find that which you are looking for, am praying for you.'' She is strict yet very loving, quite yet very opinionated and can seem sophisticated yet very humble at heart.

You certainly didn't ask for them, and you can't trade 'em, but out of the billions of human beings on our planet, they're the ones who know you best. They're the ones who cherish you, and whom you should cherish in return – whether they're your biological family or otherwise."
Tony Robbins

Other people that have been my destiny connectors are my late dad Raphael Aboka. My dad started calling me hid most intelligent beauty as soon as I was born, this helped build my confidence in many ways. My husband Norbert Griess, a man who's given up so much so many times to make sure that I have all my dreams taken care of. This man believes in me even when I feel like I'm not capable of anything. He's my biggest fan and always makes sure that I'm doing the things that I love to do and not just working for money. My brothers Nicholas, Charles, Erickson, and Franklyn have been of tremendous support through my journey in modelling, school and even in writing this book. Hopefully I'll share specific stories about them in my future writings.

Tracy and Lilian are my two youngest sisters that always feel that they need to give me the best of everything. Since I'm their eldest sister you might think that this would be my responsibility to them, yet surprisingly, they've embraced the responsibility that keeps reminding me of their love for me. My spiritual father, Bishop Mark Kegohi, has been a teacher in my life through his messages. My friends Lilian Obada and Patience Dali have also played a big role in my life. They're not only a shoulder to cry on but also my confidants in many issues.

Perhaps from listing of all my positive destiny connectors above, you were able to relate and also picture a few individuals that might play or are playing a similar role in your life. As Tony Robbins once said, we don't choose these people in our lives. They just happen to be around. They love us, support us, they know us best, and will do anything for us, we should do the same for them and others as well. We should keep our positive destiny connectors closer because there are times when we'll need them, to help us lift off the weight that we experience on our way to success from our shoulders. Let these people help you to see when you're blinded, guide you when you're off track, and challenge you when they feel you're capable of more. I've learnt so much from my fourteen-year old brother Franklyn, just as much as I have learnt from my mother or big brother Nick. Never undermine someone in your life. My point is that people around us, whom we have identified as our destiny connectors, may have as much information about the milestones we are trying to achieve or our dream profession. It's important that we consider their pieces of advice on our way to success because the road features many blunders, which gives birth to search for solutions, the need to make adjustments, joyful moments to be shared, and sorrowful moments to weep over. Don't ever think that you can always make it on that road by yourself. You'll always need people to help you through. We all have right destiny connectors, rightful and hand-picked for us. We are therefore expected to humble ourselves and learn the important lessons from these people that will direct us success.

I've seen many brilliant, talented young people who had bright futures ahead of them. Yet by neglecting their destiny connectors, they never saw the brighter side of their destiny. They're simply marking time at a level that they should have passed many years ago. I hope that you'll not make the same mistake in your life but if you have made that mistake already there's still hope for recovery. Maybe you didn't realize the importance of such people before you read this book. Well, now you know, so reconnect with those people or create newer relationships, even if it's your parents or family or spouse that you ran away from, thinking that you'd make it out there by yourself. Go back home, ask for forgiveness and pick up your dreams from where you left them. If it's your friends that betrayed you or you betrayed them, you still have a chance to return and make amends, restore your friendship, and move on with your dreams. We humans, just like any other animals, were are made to function and operate in some sort of a team spirit. Forget that going solo attitude. The moment that we isolate ourselves we quickly realize how we miss so much. Before long depression creeps in, our ability to think right and rationally gets altered, and consequently we can't concentrate on our dreams anymore.

Negative destiny connectors

Negative destiny connectors should also be kept close but we must also be wary of them. These are my other best bunch of people. They tend to try to stop you and are the complete opposite of the positive destiny connectors. They can also be your parents, siblings, friends, teachers, co-workers, spouse, fans and similar individuals in your life. You need to keep them close but always keep an eye on them. Negative destiny connectors are important to keep close because even if they're discouraging you, their actions might actually encourage you to move even higher.

When I was still a teenager, I knew that I wanted to model but had just dropped out of school following my father's death and my mother couldn't afford my school fees. One day, my neighbor told me that I would never model let alone appear in magazine. I knew that I was just a grade 11 dropout and didn't belong to a prestigious family as most models then did. All I knew was that I was daughter of the King and that in my heavenly father's house there was no luck of any kind. I knew that I'd finish high school, go to college, and pursue modelling, law or communication, which were my passions. This man's words led to me plaiting hair, saving for my examination, and facing Kenya Certificate of Secondary Education examinations two years later. Today I'm very proud to have won many local and international awards in modelling, I've travelled to places that I never thought I'd visit, and met people that I never thought I'd meet. What I'm trying to say here is that sometimes people will try to stop your dreams but you need to be your own strongest advocate to realize your dream of leading as others follow. When my neighbor was discouraging me, he didn't know he was stirring a fire within me. Similar to when Joseph's brothers sold him to the Egyptians just because they were jealous of his dreams of ruling over them, they didn't know that this wasn't a setback for Joseph but a means for him to realize his destiny.

Capable You –Everline Aboka   [93]

Joseph ended up in the palace, working for the king as a servant. He was later imprisoned after the king's wife tried to sleep with him and then falsely accused and sent to jail over allegations of rape that never took place at all. Many years later as Joseph was still a prisoner, the king had troubling dreams that only Joseph could interpret. Joseph was called upon to interpret the king's dream and after helping the king Joseph was released from prison and put in charge of the king's treasury. Joseph became a leader, and his brothers later came to him for help during a drought in that struck their homeland. From where he'd been sold years earlier, possibly sold with the intentions that him being a slave will stop his dreams from ever happening. Joseph was good man and helped his brothers with food and other produce after meeting them. Yet, if they hadn't sold Joseph as a result of them being consumed by jealousy and fearing his dreams, Joseph would never have become a leader in Egypt.

Sometimes God will put a big dream inside you but also place jealous people in your way. This helps you to move further. Know where you are planted. Discouragements that have been thrown your way can act as a boost or fertilizers in what becomes potential ground for success. Grow and never, ever think of withering, blossoming is your option. When you read Joseph's story in the bible, all you see is the humility in his eyes even though life seemed unfair to him. He didn't cry nor cursed his brothers for selling him. He didn't defend himself when the king's wife lied and accused him of rape. He accepted all these challenges and looked for a way to improve his life better at every stage of these events. Sold in slavery to work for the king, Joseph gladly worked in the palace until he was sent to prison and made his comeback as a leader in Egypt.

When we're working with our negative destiny connectors, we have to be humble and embrace their purpose in our journey. Stop complaining that they don't like you. These people are strategically placed in your life to thrust and push you toward your purpose. If you want love, you will not get it from these people. That's not their role. You obtain love from your positive destiny connectors. Your negative destiny connectors are there to provide the unfairness that will drive you even more to achieve your dream. Learn from these people and move on. Giving up on them is not an option since you can't run away from every negative destiny connectors, they are everywhere and wherever you go you will meet them or some will always follow you wherever you go, until you fulfil your God-given assignment in your race of life.

I would also like to add that negative destiny connectors can also come in the form of the misfortunes and circumstances in your life that tend to prevent you from moving forward. These situations are not meant to harm you but to prepare you for whatever dream you've been working towards. Do you know how much I miss my late father at times? Do you also know how I look back at my life to when he was alive? Recalling the care and love he offered his family and I think that if my father were still alive, I wouldn't have been the responsible woman that I am today and most probably I wouldn't have achieved all my accomplishments, including writing this book. The truth is that my father loved me and I loved him too, nobody can dispute that. Based on our close relationship it's clear that he would have been my number one fan and a positive destiny connector. However, his death was a very painful experience and it became a negative destiny connector for my life. Seeing my mother struggle to raise us after his burial made me want more, want to work harder, provide for my mom and siblings, save and invest in my future. So by the time you all say hallelujah-sweet and bitter-bye-bye to my body laying helplessly in that coffin one day, my children and husband won't be subjected to the same pain my mother, siblings and I faced when we said hallelujah- sweet and bitter-bye-bye to my daddy.

When it comes to dreams, as long as you know who's playing which roles in your connection with your destiny, you can then willingly accept your journey and focus on your goal without wasting time fighting unnecessary battles. You release control to a greater power and simply trust that even if you're thrown into a pit of lions on the road to your destiny you'll not only survive but also come out with double the power for the trouble that befell you. As long as you desire to flourish in your life, be aware that there will always be potentially painful moments. Plan not just to go through them, but soar above them, higher than the eagles in the sky because a better view of your dreams will encourage you to reach further for them. Don't stay down in a crowded place on the ground with no view at all. Regardless of what happens, soar above your challenges, because there are no crowds up above and the view is very spectacular too. Be gold and let your value increase as a result of how much fire you pass through. You can't consider being a stone, remember if the temperatures increase you'll burst and your value will be significantly reduced. Being in a level of a stone ushers you to the pain of ending up as gravel on the floor after breaking up during the heating process while probably you were meant to you were meant to build the wall of a tall tower if you were a strong unbreakable metal. You'll be covered in cement under the tower's flooring, in fact most people will not even imagine you exist because they can't see you, you are not visible, even though you'll be valuable you won't be as important as the cement that covers you or the stones that have been beautifully carved and displayed for tourists to admire and take photos of. The choice is yours. I hope that you decide to be gold and not some mere building material such as gravel. I wish you all the best as you encounter your negative destiny connectors.

Take Risks

This is one topic I love to handle with care, considering that this book targets readers from age twelve and up. The meaning of risk is totally different to a child when compared to what it means to an adult. A teenage girl that decides not to complete her homework could risk completely changing her life. Yet for a mature working class woman, calling in sick at work just to go shopping with friends in another city may not be such a big deal for her. The risks we'll examine are unconnected to these examples and are mainly concerned with achieving our goals and dreams in order to usher us into our purpose and success in life.

You see everything around us is risky, breathing in oxygen can be risky if the air is contaminated without our knowledge but we breathe it in anyway, going to bed is risky too, we never know if we would make it to the following day but we go to bed anyway, as long as we are comfortable with breathing in un clean air and going to bed without an assurance of waking up the following day, then we should not be scared about taking even bigger risks that will make us better people in life.

This mentality is what has kept me going during various frightening moments in my life. If I didn't take risks in my life, you wouldn't have known me for whom I am today. I realized that the world's most successful people all made risky choices at some point in their lives and these choices were what brought them to success.

I learned to take risks from my mother, Anna, I was barely sixteen when my father passed away. After his burial in our rural home in Alego, Siaya Kenya, I remember my uncles convincing my mother to stay with us in that rural area and not return to the rental house in Kisumu town. My mother knew that none of her children were born in the village and for that matter weren't used to a rural village life. She preferred that we merely visited our rural home and live in the town. She didn't have a job but ran a small business to sustain eleven children, including my four step siblings. Consequently, my mother had to make a choice. She could remain in the rural area where she would pay no rent, plant her own food in available family land, enroll all her children in local schools, and have a low quality of life, where even getting to hospital when sick at night would be impossible. Alternatively she could return to the rented house in Kisumu, where she'd face paying for everything, including food, rent, water, electricity, but let her children live in a familiar environment and attend their normal school. Most people would perhaps select living in the rural village where everything was free. However, my mother informed my uncles that she was going back to Kisumu, to give her children the life that her late husband had wished for. She knew that it would be hard but believed that we could push through. So we all returned to the city. She struggled to even put food on the table and there was a great deal of pain involved in this experience but today my mother's happy that she made that choice. Her main concern had been the quality of life in the village and the impact it would have on her children. She realized that most girls got married at an early age or had children before their fourteenth birthday. The boys joined community gangs, used drugs, and didn't care about education. Today all my mother's children have a college education of some sort except for her youngest son, Franklyn, who enrolled into high school in 2015, the same year that this book was written.

On our way to success we'll also be faced with situations where we'll have to choose the most difficult situation over the simplest situation. Difficult moments allow us to learn and grow, so we should embrace situations that initially appear to be problematic because either way we have to grow in order to move forward.

I always did something I was a little not ready to do. I think that's how you grow. When there's that moment of 'Wow, I'm not really sure I can do this,' and you push through those moments, that's when you have a breakthrough."
Marissa Mayer

To reach our highest potential, we should have an "I can" attitude and 'I'm in'' attitude. We aren't going to learn new things if we don't try them out. That's what taking risk is all about. This is your life. You have to stand out and be persistent in everything that you do. Only you can make your life better, so aspire to stand out and not just to fit in. If success was easy you'd be surrounded by successful people everywhere but it aren't. Only one in a thousand or more people that you meet is a doctor, author, banker, astronaut, or other notable professional and the rest are just ordinary people. We're so worried about what others will think of us when we do certain things. Some of us even believe that success and riches are related to dark forces that they don't want to be associated with it in anyway. However, you're not going to get anywhere in life if you care too much about your reputation. Sometimes you just need to think beyond what others might believe or say about you.

I recently appeared on a television series set with another young woman from Africa. We were shooting in a private home in Alberta. The home was spectacular worth $14 million Canadian dollars. I shared my love of that house with this woman but she told me that she'd never wish to have such a house for herself. She felt that it was wrong for one person to own such a home while many people were homeless. This made sense to me and homelessness is an issue that touches my heart. Yet I felt that she was placing so many limitations on reaching a dream of owning such a home based on the values of a society, on problems caused by the society and should be solved by the society. I could see clearly in her eyes that she'd never risk owning such a home because her beliefs would work against her. Maybe you have the same mentality? Perhaps you believe that wealth is sin and having wealth in itself is sin or something else prevents you from succeeding financially. Try being very poor and you'll be surprised at how sinful people will perceive you are. They'll say that you sinned and that's why you're poor and can't enjoy any blessings in life. I believe that so much has been given to us. We have the key to success and to the abundant lifestyle that we desire to live. All we need to do is take a risk in believing that this is possible and work hard to achieve these things in our lives.

Clear your mind and refresh the way in which you view success and prosperity. Walk, breath, speak, sleep, and live it and you'll be surprised at how far you can get with anything that you set your mind to. If your family believes that achieving something in life is sinful, go ahead and achieve that which you want to achieve. I'm not recommending that you be disrespectful to people who adore such negative belief systems. All you need to know is that this is your life. If you fail people will talk about your failure and if you succeed they'll still talk anyway. Why wait for them to talk about your loss while you can instead make them talk about your success? You

know what you want in your life. As long as you're
not killing anyone on your way to make your dreams
come true, then go for it. Once you get that one scary
move going, you'll never encounter any kind of fear
and before you know it you'll be an expert in risk
taking. I don't know of anything that gets and sounds
better than this as you work your way up the ladder of
achieving your dreams.

Be full of gratitude

Many people fail to come into direct contact with
their dreams not because they are never fulfilled but
just because they are too focused on what was not
happening. As a result they miss the opportunity to
celebrate the joy of those dreams that that did happen
to them. There's so much that can happen to us when
we take time to be thankful about everything in our
lives. I find that gratitude is a magnet that attracts
even more success, opportunities, blessings, and
abundance.

*"Be thankful for what you have; you'll end up having
more. If you concentrate on what you don't have, you
will never, ever have enough." - Oprah Winfrey*

The gratitude that we should concentrate on is that which appreciates us as individuals, appreciates others, appreciates the existence of a greater being in our lives, and appreciates our environment and ecosystem as well. During all my years of keeping fit I've learnt to thank my body after every workout for having been able to manage the stress of the exercise routine without giving up. It's this simple move from my side that makes my body feel that it's appreciated and encouraged to engage in the next workout. If my long limbs start to hurt later in the day, I remember to say a few words of encouragement to this body, which helps speed up the healing process. I thank my long legs for every runway walk and all the long hours they spend doing endless tiring photo shoots. Even right now I'm thanking my mind for the ideas it's given and keeps giving me as I continue to write this book. The same applies to my fingers that are typing the words and my eyes that are alert to detect any spelling and spacing mistakes. Remaining thankful has been proven to help us release tension in times of trouble, a state of mind that our body truly appreciates especially when we're climbing the ladder to success and encountering very challenging situations.

How to stay thankful in life

For us to remain thankful, we all need to know how to do this, even when circumstances tell us that it's time to do the complete opposite. We live in a world where our media feed us so much bad news that it's difficult to maintain positivity or gratitude. We require a few guidelines if we're to perform to the fullest.

Have a gratitude list

It's easier to stay thankful when we write down a list of the things that we're thankful for in our lives. Anyone can create such a list. Mine includes things that I'm grateful for every morning when I wake up. They range from things that cost nothing but are worth the whole world to me to material items that I can put value on. My list includes my life, mother, siblings, husband, children (yes they are coming), oxygen, love, peace, health, trust, opportunities, dreams achieved and yet to be achieved, favor, blessing, joy, food, housing, clothing, pets, car, gadgets and more.

Share your gratitude with others

If we keep telling people things are very bad in our lives we end up feeling bad and depressed. Similarly, we'll feel good when we tell people about the things in our lives about which we're thankful for. Over the years I've learnt to tell people how thankful I am that my husband is part of my life. The more I did this the more I realized that we stay happier around each other, our love blossoms and we have a happy marriage.

Stay positive all the time

We can't be thankful if our minds are filled with negativity. We have to maintain a positive attitude for us to better appreciate this life. If you want to get into the habit of being thankful for your parents then you must start viewing them as important and wonderful individuals and not as old fashion people with inferior knowledge on just about everything.

Be Content

Contentment is not difficult to achieve in life. Perhaps you don't have shoes now but are thankful to have two legs. Maybe you haven't been able to get a promotion at work but be thankful that you have a job. Perhaps you haven't achieved yet all your dreams but are thankful that you're not where you were a year ago. Maintaining this type of mentality stops us from complaining as we wait for the rain of abundance to fall on us. We all have dreams of finishing school, getting married, getting a promotion and so on, but we should learn to give thanks. For example, I'm working hard to buy my new home but in the meantime am happy in my current house. Many people confuse contentment with a lack of vision or ambition in life but I say knowing that a being bigger than you is in control of your life and not you, He has directed good favors your way and is working behind the scenes to take you to your divine destiny.

In life we shouldn't take for granted the opportunities and blessings around us, but when we're discontented that's exactly what we do. We're focused so much on what we want to happen in the future that we fail to acknowledge what we have and should be enjoying right now.

Lack of contentment leads us into a valley of frustration and depression. If we're not watchful, these two major vices will keep us where we are, force us to remain stagnant, and not experience any growth in our lives. If we don't learn to master contentment in our difficult moments, we're not likely to be content when we reach our dreams. If all we do is complain during hard times, we'll experience the same thing even if we achieve our big dreams. Discontentment, like any other vice, can follow us all our lives, so the earlier we learn to deal with it the better. I've always noticed that the unhappy people I meet don't seem to appreciate anything in life. It sometimes seems as if I meet these people everywhere I go and you probably do too. You need to watch out for them because their spirits and character traits can transfer to you so easily and you don't want to deal with that. It's amusing, annoying, and ridiculous that dark skinned people use skin lightening products to be lighter while lighter skinned people get tanned to become darker. People with no hair spend so much money on fake hair while those that possess hair chop it all off. Overweight people spend all their life in the gym shedding weight, while their paperweight counterparts are always searching for ways to gain weight. Single people can't be happy until they're married and married people don't seem to want anything to do with their marriages anymore. What is happening to the human race? Why is everybody looking for something they don't have instead of being content with their bodies? What I say to the single people is whatever you do learn to enjoy your single status because once you're married you'll long to be single even again but there will be no going back. That's the reality of marriage. You won't read about in the ''happily ever after'' bridal magazines and books. This is craziness that's prevalent in the world in which we live in. If you consider all your friends you'll realize that they've all experienced some form of discontentment, but having read this book you should be the agent of change in your associations. Let your friends learn from you all the good values contained in this book.

Help yourself by helping others

All my life, whenever I want encouragement that will give me a greater appreciation of life I tend to go to hospitals, homeless centers, or centers for the disabled. When I see a disabled man writing with his feet holding a pen, I then realize that I should be thankful for my hands and also be grateful that I can hold the paper and pen. Helping the nurse with a patient who is so sick that she can't turn herself helps me appreciate that I'm still energetic and healthy enough to turn around on my own bed.

Focus on your strengths not your weaknesses

Sometimes we beat ourselves so hard for not achieving what we intended when we should be focusing on what we actually achieved not what we didn't, concentrating on our strengths not our weaknesses. I am yet to meet a person that has no weaknesses. We all have weaknesses, even those people that present themselves as perfect have weaknesses too. Every time I read my bible, I realize how mighty men of God that He used to perform various miracles had some significant weaknesses in their lives. One day Moses was a murderer the following day he was leading God's people to the Promised Land. Noah was building the ark that saved God's creation from flooding and the next day he was drunk and running around naked. One day Peter was performing miracles and healing people and the next day he was denying Christ. Judas was a very good disciple of Christ but then he was betraying Christ just to have a few pennies. And you think you have weaknesses and that you're the biggest sinner alive? Think again! You haven't seen weaknesses yet!

Without our weaknesses and mistakes we can't learn enough to prepare for our divine destiny. Mistakes happen so that we can learn from them. Let them mold you but don't dwell on them. Holding onto mistakes will hold you back so much that you'll never reach your destiny. Some people still remember the things they did or that happened to them in kindergarten and even worse they claim it's the reason why they can't reach their highest potential in life. I heard a story about a man in his seventies who was bullied in high school by his fellow students at a science symposium. The man did an amazing job at that event and even won an award from his project in this symposium. His closest competitor was famous in school but didn't win an award. He organized his friends to attack the young man who'd won. They told him that he was stupid and not capable and from that day forward the man believed he couldn't do anything right. He blamed himself for winning an award that caused him so much pain and he never participated in any academic competitions again, even though it wasn't his fault that he was treated poorly. He made the mistake of dwelling so much on what had happened over sixty years earlier in high school that even today he's not moving forward. He's still focused on those errors from the past that he should have learnt from and let go of many years ago

If we focus on our weaknesses, they're all that we'll see. If you're going for your driver's test and you remember the humiliation you felt when you failed your previous one, you run the risk of not passing again, despite having spent so much time studying for it. Learn to see and dwell on the instances when you did something amazingly and were successful. This is what helped me to surmount rejection in the modelling industry. Whenever I contested for a title and didn't win, such as the M-Net Face of Africa at the Africa competition level, I encouraged myself with the two previous awards that I'd won unopposed. Today even with the knowledge of how biased the modelling industry can be, I thank myself so much for having performed far and beyond my capabilities to have all these awards. Those moments didn't kill me, but rather made me grow. I arrived at a point where whenever I faced rejection, especially in North America where racism presents itself as more common, I'd tell myself, "They don't know what they're going to miss without me on their team because I'm unique, talented, and highly favored. I'm the best deal, my face or long legs alone can sell a product to millions around the globe. It's their loss for not having me on board."

Armed with all this information about focusing on your strengths, you're the only one that can steer your ship in the desired direction. If you want to sail south where you may not survive because you're busy dwelling on your weaknesses, you have only yourself to blame. If you sail north, motivate yourself by focusing on your strengths. You can still applaud and be proud of yourself at the end of the day. So south or north, each time the choice is all yours, come rain or shine.

Dare to dream even bigger

Studies show that most old people on their deathbeds mourn not just about the things they did but also those that they didn't during the time they had. It's a shame but it's too late. The death bell has rung and they have to depart. Nobody wants to be in this situation. I personally don't want to live a mediocre life so that when my time comes I mourn about that book that I knew I wanted to write since I was a teenager but I didn't. Or that motivational speech I wanted to share with young people about life but I never gave. I want to go to my rest knowing that I did all that I could do with the opportunities that I had. Then I'll realize that I lived my life fully. This is my life. I run the show and I'm in control. All I do is what feels right in my heart.

I've come to accept that when you have a dream, people will often laugh at you. They'll wonder if about your idiocy levels. They'll tell you to be realistic with your dreams but I've realized that this is always an excuse for pessimist. When an idea is planted in our hearts and minds, only we have the vision of that idea. Others may possess the sense of sight of it but they can't clearly see what has been planted in our hearts because they lack that vision to view the idea in our mind. At this point I let people's words go in one ear and out through the other.

Our minds can be compared to wine skins. They can contain a great deal of wine when they're new but when they become old, the wine skin is hard and useless. It's important for us to frequently renew our minds as far as our dreams and other aspirations are concerned. Get into the habit of thinking and expecting larger dreams to take place. The bible states that the path of the righteous grows brighter and brighter. God's plan for us is that we may live a bigger life, become more influential and so on. It is up to us to run from mediocrity and pursue greatness. We can't let it become an accepted part of our lives. We need to rise up to attain a life of overflow and abundance. We can't allow the enemy to constantly contain us when God's intention is to bless, lift and enlarge us.

Most of the time we disappoint our God or the universe depending on your personal beliefs. That bigger power within you has always reminded you of how capable you are, but we often let our environment of mediocrity consume us. We tend to believe that we resemble our fathers, grandfathers, or other ancestors. Yet we forget that although these people might have lived in mediocrity that doesn't mean that we should feel comfortable and settle where they did in life. What if you're the difference maker in your family? Maybe where you come from a place where nobody has been educated beyond a high school level. Perhaps you don't have sufficient food and having three meals a day has never happened in your family. Maybe you can't afford much, don't have school supplies, or your family can't pay for vacations because you can't afford it. Everything in life seems like a luxury that your family can't afford. I want you to know that you're reading this book because that bigger power inside you has appointed you to be the one who'll break your family's cycle of poverty and mediocrity. It only takes one person in a family to usher the other coming generations into the land of abundance. That happens when they realize their purpose in their family, accepting the responsibility of thinking bigger and moving far and beyond what their environment dictates that they can achieve.

When you decide to follow your dreams you will witness them becoming reality, it's advisable to set the bar even higher the next time you approach that task. If your dream was to excel in your career, consider continuing until you reach the upper management level and don't be think about remaining at the subordinate or maintenance level. If it's going to take more schooling to enter upper management go for it and stop at nothing. Growing up in the slums of Nyalenda, I knew in my heart that, that was not where I wanted to spend the rest of my life. The challenges I faced there helped to shape my future but at no point did I want to spend my life in an environment where everything was lacking and the crime rate was increasing with each passing day. When life threw me a curve and voices screamed at me that I had to stay there, I decided to work my way up the ladder. I made steady progress with my schooling, modelling and work, moving ever closer to getting out of that place. This might have been a suitable location for my mom to raise us but I realized that somehow, somebody had to remove that Nyalenda mentality from my family and that's what I did. I may now be living far away from my family and friends but I'm glad that I seized the opportunity of dreaming beyond the Nyalenda slums.

Don't be afraid to dream bigger. Go for it, my friend and stop waiting for somebody in your family or community to do it. They may never do it and the worst that could happen is living in that cycle of mediocrity until goodness knows when!

If you're going to be the first person to have a white wedding in your mother's family line, like I did in 2011, go for it. If you happen to be the first to move from your town to another town or country to seek better opportunities, go for it. Should you happen to own the first car in your community and have the flexibility of not using public transit all the time, go for it, if you happen to be the one to start an organization that will bring change in your community and improve the lives of many, go for it. Should you be the one to say no to drugs and alcoholism in your family so that those that come after you don't have their lives ruined because of alcohol, go for it. If you're the girl that's going to break the cycle of teenage pregnancy and giving birth before marriage in your family and community, go for it. Should you happen to be the first person in your village to build a stone house, go for it. And if you happen to be the very first in your family and

*community to graduate with honors from a university,
go ahead and do it.*

As long as whatever you do in your bigger dreams improves your life and the lives of people around you, by all means go for it. The universe is up for grabs and you have a great chance in this game, so all the best as you get on a journey to achieving your bigger dreams.

Successfully use hints from your family history to better your own life

The dreams of my father, Raphael Aboka.
"The best way to live a successful life is to not only prioritize what should be done now, but being bold enough to decide and not to let other conflicting factors distract you."

The above words have remained with me since my teenage years and I also believe that these are words that my siblings can relate to. As my late father constantly reminded us of the same words.

"Take your time right now to study, to make a better life for yourself in the future and to not allow yourselves to be distracted by the pleasures your peers are involved in today. There is no end to a pleasurable life, as you grow older you will realize that new forms of pleasure keep trending. If you choose the way of pleasure and expensive lifestyles you will soon notice that all your money and investments are depleted but pleasure is still as it was if not increasing in numbers. Pleasure cannot be depleted, your money will be"

By now you might be thinking that I was lucky to be raised by a wise man and I can confirm that. My father, and my mother are the original carriers of the genes of tenacity and determination that my siblings and I are grateful to have flowing through our veins today. At the age of ten, my father found himself entangled in a family crisis when his mother fled for her ancestry home fleeing from a dysfunctional marriage. She was the fifth of the seven wives to my grandfather, a renowned and rich catechist of Umala, location, Karemo division of Siaya district in Nyanza,

Kenya. Despite the painful challenges of growing up in one stepmother's house after another, by class five, my father managed to keep attending school and eventually sat for his final primary school education. Proceeded to high school and he later received training as a mechanical engineer specializing in building pumping water systems that served the greater south Nyanza arid regions of Kenya. At his time of death my father had worked for Lake Basin Development Authority, a branch of Ministry of Minerals and Natural Resources, for almost three decades, a significant achievement considering that he passed away when he was only 44 years old. My siblings and I remember our father as a success-oriented man that not only pushed us to achieve so much for ourselves but also believed that we could achieve it. He shared with us how he wanted all of his children not to miss out on a university education like he did. How all the new hires in his company would pass through him for six months full-time training and later they'd pass the tests of their probation hire period. In most cases they'd gain a promotion to higher levels in the company while my father would maintain the same position, earning the same amount of money for many years simply because he had no university degree. From this experience my dad understood the power of education in Kenya and invested most of his earnings to give us the best education by enrolling us in some of the best schools and supporting every bit of our study needs. He wished to get a promotion, to work abroad like many of new employees that he trained did later on, get us all to study overseas and take us out of a life of mediocrity. And yet perhaps that life was purposefully placed in our lives to build, shape and strengthen us especially after his death. If it hadn't been placed there I wouldn't have been able to write this book and my siblings wouldn't continue to shine in their achievements.

My father constantly used himself and his brother as a reminder to us that success is achievable, despite what sometimes appear to be insurmountable challenges. His brother, Honorable Otieno Mc Onyango, former Member of Parliament of Siaya County in the late 1980's and early 1990's. My uncle

Otieno rose from the same background as my father and became an editor for Standard News Paper in Kenya. However in 1982 he was arrested with Hon. Raila Amollo Odinga, the former Kenyan prime minister, and became a political prisoner, charged with attempting to overthrow President Daniel Toroitich Arap Moi in the coup that took place that year. After several years in prison, during which he was denied visits from most family members except my father and a few others, my uncle used the pain that he'd suffered in prison to launch his political career later on after gaining his freedom. He later served Siaya County, Kenya as a member of parliament for a decade.

He served two terms in the parliament for a maximum of ten years. We all grew up as siblings knowing that we could achieve so much just as dad and uncle. We all knew that there had been people before us that had shone in their achievements, that itself was and is still a torch of hope for us. A keen observation of your family history can help you discover the inspiration to escape from your mediocre environment and achieve extraordinary success. Examine the history and if you see brokenness declare that, that is a motivation for you. My father ran from one stepmother's house to another in order to survive when he was only a child. My uncle was a political prisoner, separated from his family and denied his freedom. I was a child that grew up in the womb that faced two severe uterine bleeding episodes after my mom conceived me. I had no school fees in grade 11 but the challenges and hardships my family members and I experienced didn't stop us. In fact these encouraged us to want to see more of that other side of success. Keep your head high, keep dreaming, and don't stop until the giant of mediocrity is dead and rotting under your feet.

Chapter Three
That Successful You

By now you've done everything possible and are living your dream life of success, so what's next? This is the biggest question that many people don't ask themselves on their journey up the ladder but it's also a very important part of the process. Do you ever wonder why some artists make so much money at the peak of their career and then later end up living on the streets or in utter poverty later on? This is because at the height of success many of them failed to ask themselves this question ''what's next after I achieve success?'' After they made their way to success, they didn't know what to do with themselves. Many faced a situation where they felt they'd already lived their best days and there was nothing much to pursue in the future. Unfortunately they used everything they had carelessly and eventually all their money was depleted. Their bank saving accounts read zero while the rapture nor the end of the world hadn't yet occurred.

This is a very bad situation in which to find yourself after many years of hard work. This is why the majority of such people that don't plan ahead face so much depression that they end up committing suicide, either by drugging themselves to their death beds or other means. You're a wonderful talent and worker and fortunately, because you have all this wonderful information about what's right and not right from this book, you're well equipped and prepared for your destiny to enjoy life after achieving your success.

You'll realize that some things that you need to do after success are those that you've perhaps done before yet still have to do again. Don't worry because that's what life is about, routines that are either daily or seasonal. There's no escape. Live your success well.

Live successfully.

Living a successful life can be categorized into three familiar steps. I like to say Life= Laugh often + Love always + Live now. These three are the most fundamental human needs. It may look easy to achieve yet it can still represent a steep mountain for many to climb.

Laugh often

Most importantly, be happy. At the end of the day that's what life's all about. Let the joy that comes from your appreciation of life within and without be evident in your aura all the time.

Experience pleasure

If you've discovered something that brings long term pleasure to your body, soul and mind, consider that a treasured chicken soup for your soul on a cold snowy day to ease your flu and cold symptoms and **experience it with gratitude**. You may have noticed that I've used the words ''**experience with gratitude''** in bold. This is because I know of a few people that enjoy the right pleasures, some engage in safe and long-term fulfilling pleasures while others prefer the one minute pleasure that will ultimately lead to disaster in their lives. You must realize that while eating chocolate may bring you pleasure, it can also be very harmful to your health used excessively.

Driving your sports car at a fast and furious speed may be fun on a hot summer afternoon but losing a leg, arm or dying isn't pleasurable at all.

Love always: Relationship and network magic

Friends, family and even strangers are worthy of your affection. Showing affection and receiving or reciprocating that same affection is a basic human need that we should all have to learn from the beginning of our school years but unfortunately we're not taught this important lesson. There's a certain kind of magic and power in love. We must all learn to tap into this magic and not allow the world to draw us away from it. A man or woman receiving or reciprocating love is said to be happier, healthier, and more successful than their counterparts that have none of such advantages.

Because love is such an important aspect of our daily life, many businesses and individuals have used hatred to poison the hearts of many people, telling them that there is no such thing as love. Such people have no interest in making you a better person. Their mission is to see you rot in loneliness and depression until you die. Good examples your family member that's telling you to quit your marriage, or your lawyer that's constantly reminding you to serve your spouse with divorce papers because he or she feels that your marriage has hit an iceberg has no good intentions for your happiness. As these people keep pushing you out of a relationship that your heart tells you is right. None of these outside parties know the affection that you feel for your spouse, regardless of the painful moments that you've both encountered. A good piece of advice to those facing a difficult time with relationships is to ask the couple to seek counselling and work on their marriage. By now you're probably saying it's all cool because the government allows divorce, so what's the big deal in signing those papers? Let me remind you that for decades the government has fed you genetically modified foods and as a result you're obese, suffer from high blood pressure, diabetes, or cancer but you still trust the damn government. Every government comes into power determined to push its own agenda and very little in that agenda concerns you. Be smart, be vigilant, be full of integrity and let your heart be the one to make choices of love on your behalf, not the government. When your state has weak conditions for divorce, step back, think twice and ask yourself why the government is giving you an easier way to your loneliness.

Have you ever asked yourself why the government will not show you plainly how and why to love but is very quick to tell you how, why, and when you should divorce? The more lonely and depressed you are, the more likely you can be manipulated by any system. Remember, when we're talking about success, we're talking about taking charge of our thoughts over manipulation, ideas and experience. Choose wisely and always choose love because love keeps the heart beating.

Be observant

We have the unique power to observe our lives and decide to spend more time doing what we want to do and less doing what we don't want to do. It's very important to discover our purpose, vision, and mission if we want to get the most out of life and to realize our true potential during our lifetimes. The land will always be conquered by the learners and observant.

Love books

Every problem that you'll ever face in life has already been conquered by someone else. The solution to these problems have been documented in books. One of the things that I advise my clients to do is to devise their own learning budget. Whatever you're earning try to spend between ten and fifteen percent of that on books, success programs, and personal development workshops, or something that motivates you, so that you can dream, discover and to live your passion. Try this and see the magical rise in your bank balance as a result of your intelligent choices. Your mind will never function at optimum level unless you feed it good material to read and contemplate. Fiction novels, thrillers, and mommy-porn never benefit your health, relationships and finances. In fact they only worsen your condition.

Be yourself

You only have one life so make sure that you don't waste a single moment of your time living someone else's life or dreams. Love others but make sure no one loves you more than you love yourself. Don't seek social approval for things that are morally right and important to you. You must prefer loneliness over immoral company. Be completely at peace with yourself. If you have feelings of guilt about your past then forgive yourself and make a fresh start.

Serve people

Your success is measured by the size of the contribution you make to the world. Only human beings can go beyond themselves and serve the humanity. Treat the entire world like your family. Share your happiness with people and help them to overcome their sorrows and weaknesses. A good life is a life of service.

Live now

I've made it a habit not to worry about things that are out of my control. Instead I've used the time to reevaluate my life and work on the things that I can change as opposed to those that I can't. It's pointless for me to worry about tomorrow's bad weather. All I can do is dress in layers, pack lots of warm food, and keep my day running. I can't control the weather but I can surely control the fact that I can work and stay productive on a chilly day by dressing so warmly that I can barely feel the pain of the cold.

Spirituality

Regardless of whether you believe in the existence of a superior being or not, it's been proven that a good number of successful people have a relationship with a being that's superior to themselves. For us to wake up and retire safely to bed every single day, it takes a power larger than us to control and make all things possible. Every morning before I jump out of bed, I offer myself to a being greater than myself, seeking blessings that this being takes control of the day and allows me to live it successfully.

Health

Keep yourself mentally and physically fit. Spare one hour every day for yourself and ensure you work out for a minimum of 30 minutes every day. You should also meditate for 30 minutes every day, 15 minutes in the morning and 15 minutes before you retire to bed. Physical workouts build your muscle mass and keep your metabolism healthy. Meditation cleanses and cleans you internally and is also proven to help build your empathy. We certainly need more empathic than arrogant people in the world today. An individual that's chosen the path to exercising, a healthy diet, and meditation is the enemy of the health insurance companies. They can only admire your money from afar but they can't get their hands on it because your life's free of sickness.

Master Public Speaking

Public speaking is the fastest way to build self-confidence and in public speaking there's always something new to learn and explore. People with the ability to speak confidently receive faster promotions in their professional lives. They also have more customers and are perceived as natural leaders by people around them. I'm yet to meet a great public speaker that's poor in his or her life. Public speaking is a skill that anyone that's willing to learn can master.

Procrastination

If you have to procrastinate then you must procrastinate the act of procrastination itself.

Time is the fabric that our lives are made of and is a much more valuable resource than money. Time cannot be saved and it can only be invested in meaningful activities or wasted in useless pursuits. Never wait for the right time to begin a right thing otherwise else you'll always be waiting. Your tomorrow is determined by what you do today.

Take Action

All goals fail without action. Action is the difference between the Warren Buffet you know and the Simon Buffet you've never heard of. Hard work will always beat talent. Maintain a daily schedule and then follow it religiously. Observe your actions and improve them every day. Fall in love with taking action and the rewards will take care of themselves

Moderation

Try doing everything in moderation. Too much of something is said to be dangerous even if it's something that you feel will be of great help and importance to you. Go easy on the number of cups of coffee, and the amount of food or alcohol that you consume in a day, as well as the total amount of time you spend studying, working, working out, meditating, and so on.

These are a few guiding principles that could help you enjoy your success after many years and months of working hard toward it.

Re-evaluate your goals – Move forward not backward

Without reevaluation after achieving a certain goal, stagnation is inevitable. We have to constantly feed our brains with new ideas or else we can't grow.

In chapter two, we explored how we can design goals that are both straightforward and achievable. In this chapter, we'll do the same, but this time we have to be very keen on moving forward but not backward to grow from where we were to where we want to go. Timothy was a manager at a communication company when he learned of his ability and power to change everything around his life. After studying this self-philosophy for a while he knew he wanted more from life than just being a departmental manager. He would stop at nothing until he achieved his goal that would make him better, smarter, richer, healthier, powerful, and in control.

As you've noticed by now, many things that we fail to accomplish in life don't occur that way because somebody hates us or somebody prevented our goals from happening. We control what happens to us by what we constantly declare and think about. Our futures aren't shaped in a family environment, school, or religion but in our brains. All those aspects may provide the other factors, but the life of our dreams happens in our brains. When I say brain, I don't mean the ''brainy'' aspect of the brain, but am referring to that one organ that every human being has. For that reason, you don't have to be the smartest in your school, team, or family to realize your potential in life. All you need to do is to drop the pictures of how you'd like your life to happen into your brain, work hard towards seeing the reality of that picture and watch the rest unfold. It's as simple as that, with no rocket science involved.

Timothy started working for the company as an administrative assistant immediately after completing his two-year diploma course in business administration. Even though he'd moved up the ladder reasonably quickly five years after graduation, he wanted to pursue his degrees at the university level, move up the ladder to the role of chief executive officer, and own his communications company. He enrolled for his university education, working at his managerial position at the communication's company and studying part time, mainly evenings and weekends, in a two-year program. One year into the program, Timothy's boss, the chief executive officer, quit because his wife was transferred to a job in another city. The company board of directors started searching for a replacement for the outgoing chief executive officer. They learned that Timothy had enrolled in a university program that would put him in a better position as a candidate for the prole. After a series of interviews and consultations among the board of directors, they unanimously made a decision to offer Timothy the position, even though he was only halfway through with his degree course in business management. Timothy accepted the offer, graduated from his program the following year and worked as a chief executive for the company. He then started his communications company after three more years, where he continues to work hard to not only put his company on the corporate map but also increase his income with each passing year. I was astonished to learn that Timothy had maintained his humility throughout his journey. He's also working with various organizations to improve the lives of children in developing countries. Timothy understands how much a child might benefit from his experience of always looking around for help after losing both of his parents in a road accident that he and his two younger sisters survived when he was only six years old. Just like Timothy, most of us should know that we have the ability to plan our lives ahead of various successes in life. We can't wait until an opportunity presents itself. Let the opportunity come and find you ready, even if you're not even halfway up the ladder of your dreams. Just as in writing professions, the employer always wants to meet a candidate that has a portfolio of his or her work ready. In most cases it doesn't matter how little work you have to show someone. The fact that they can see it indicates that you enjoy writing, which also gives you more points than another candidate that initially appears to be more capable but has nothing to show for it.

Steps to goals re-evaluation

Change of priorities

It's common to have changing priorities in life. We think and visualize things and the more we do this, the more we'll experience this in our lives. The change in priorities can guide us through the process of reevaluation of our goals. Maybe you were planning to own a summer vacation home in Florida but you just had a wonderful opportunity of starting a booming business in Nairobi, Kenya? At this point you'll need to assess the importance of being present at your company at the crucial conception stage or just move to Florida and continue with the purchase of your dream house at the expense of the money that you've already invested in your new company.

Next dream

We can go about this by asking ourselves, "What is my next dream, now that I've achieved success in my previous goals?"

I've noticed that some brave people have a tendency to write big goals, perhaps because we think that they'll not come to pass soon and that they will have time to pass with it. Unfortunately, dreams come true in most cases after you start working hard on them and after that we're expected to go back to the drawing board and come up with new ideas that can help us move forward. If you've realized that you currently have breakfast in Beijing, China, and dinner in New York, United States of America, as a result of a goal you've been tirelessly working towards, it's now time to challenge yourself with another goal that will surpass the one that you've already achieved. How about breakfast in Paris, France, and dinner in Rabat, Morocco, two days a week, in my private jet? Not too big of a goal, very straightforward and achievable.

Unexpected new interests

When we start to experience an interest in doing something that we were once not so keen about, it's definitely time to adjust the gears and move appropriately. I want to make it clear that before you make any adjustments when in this state, it's very important to take note of the impact of this new interest in your life. Avoid moving merely for the sake of your desires, wicked or not. Make sure that your new interests are in line with your values and beliefs and are socially acceptable according to the law of your country. For example if you are an English student at the university it's still considered a good move to pursue your new interests in speech pathology. These are connected and each can lead to achieving the other, as opposed to dropping out of school altogether and failing to graduate. Dropping out of school may be a new interest but bear in mind that it won't usher you into being better. Sometimes it might just take away the little good you have built over the years.

A dairy farmer that's been adamant about keeping a goat for its milk might have an interest in doing so after realizing that there's a lucrative market for the product. For this reason that's a new interest worth investing more time and resources in.

Bucket list

By this time if you probably hadn't thought about achievements and accomplishments to realize before you kick the bucket, this is the time to do so. We are all mortal. We can't avoid death but we can make plans to live a fulfilling life in the time frame entrusted to us. Maybe at this stage you think that you don't have more goals and you've achieved all that you wanted to achieve. I challenge you to go back and draft or redraft your bucket list. Believe me, there must be something out there that still needs your attention. As long as you're still inhaling oxygen and exhaling carbon dioxide, the reality of life demands that you have something to add in your list. Please don't add death, just because I have reminded you to add something. Make it something better.

I love bucket lists. I have quite interesting stuff on mine, including climbing Mount Kilimanjaro and Mount Kenya before I'm thirty five years old, writing and changing lives through my books, building a rescue home for street children in Kenya, having an exceptional vacation with my mother and siblings, and taking a break from everything to travel around the world in one year. Bucket lists are a very powerful motivation in life. They push you to look forward and achieve those very goals in your life. You don't need a bucket list filled with huge goals. The list contain items as simple as sharing your food with neighbors or street dwellers once a month. I do feel that the more this list involves others, the greater the difference we'll make and greater the contentment we'll experience.

Involve your instincts

"Do stuff, be clenched, curious. Not waiting for inspiration's shove or society's kiss on your forehead. Pay attention. It's all about paying attention, attention is vitality. It connects you with others. It makes you eager, stay eager." - Susan Sontag

I love my instincts. They're my best friends. At least they've never lied to me but I've had to face difficult situations whenever I've refused to obey them. You may believe that I'm a slave to my instincts but I accept this slavery because it doesn't put me in chains forever. Rather my instincts usher me into the realm of possibilities, anointing, blessings, and comfort by untying me from the bondages of fear, mediocrity, and shame.

The moment that you feel as if your instincts are leading you to a new adventure, be still and know that the time has finally come for you to reevaluate your life goals, regardless of how comfortable you are with your current life. It's a situation that only involves two choices. You can choose to do as your instincts direct, after weighing all your options and realizing the benefits that the opportunity will present you and people around you. Or you may choose not to follow your instincts and so miss out on the fun adventure ahead of you. Let's imagine that you might have finished working on your college business diploma. You hear a deep conviction about not accepting any job offer that's going to pay you the salary you could make in a day should you choose to start your own business instead. This might be a tough decision but you're as good as dead when you fail to make the right decision or even fail to decide at all. Not accepting a job offer may be the hardest decision you'll be faced with, especially considering that throughout your schooldays you heard teachers, parents, and mentors stress the importance of getting a job after completing your education. Ever realized that just a few individuals will acknowledge that you can create wealth out of a talent or a simple business? If you feel that starting a business is the way to go do your homework, know what's required, and if you feel satisfied with the benefits of starting your own business, go for it. After all, all employers know that spending more than forty hours a week employing you just makes you more tired, denying you the opportunities to keep pursuing your bigger goals.

Bold enough to move forward

The main reason we're looking at the steps to reevaluating our dreams is that we can be bold enough to move beyond fear into uncharted territories. For most people fear is the number one factor in the inability to do anything. The spirit of fear reminds you that you're incapable. I'm here to tell you that you're capable of anything, including defeating that same fear that presents itself as a threat to you. We have to persist in moving forward. We can't just allow anything to hold us back! This isn't a request but something we should hold onto dearly as an unbreakable command. The choice is all ours as change begins with us all the time.

Once you've realized your bravery in continuing to move forward, go for it! There's no time to waste as the time machine never waits for you. The second, minute, hour, day, week, month, and year handles of the clock keeps moving regardless of whether you choose to move or remain stagnant, so why not just move with it? Move forward. I don't care how you want to go about it. If crawling is the easiest way, move. If it's flying, keep moving and keep moving. I recently asked my friend that had just earned his master's in engineering if he would study more. He told me that moving forward is a priority for him as long as he lives. I felt good in my spirit because I knew that my visions and attributes were at least rubbing off in my friend's life. It made me feel that my constant reminders to him to stay positive weren't in vain but were bearing more fruits than I'd envisioned.

Stay in touch with your destiny connectors
In chapter two we examined the idea of our destiny connectors and you were probably wondering what to do with them once you've achieved your very first goals. Well, they're just as important on this journey

again. Remember they could also be your source of inspiration and strength on your new journey.

"A dream you dream alone is only a dream. A dream you dream together is reality."
John Lennon

We all know the power of connections. Merely by sharing a dream with the right people you can find yourself smoothly sailing through your goals because you know people who have your back regardless of how fearful you are. They offer you a shoulder to lean on and wipe your tears throughout the journey. At times our ego tells us that we don't need this kind of a connection. However, our bodies, dreams, and goals are too big for such an ego, so drop it down and embrace the power of people around you in a more incredible way than ever before. We all made it into this world through our biological parents and the fact remains that in every other step of our lives after birth we still need people around. Think about it. To learn how to cry you need that nurse attending to your mom at delivery to gently spank you or pinch you if you can't cry on your own. I know you're wondering why that nurse still remains a connection worth keeping in touch with after she decided to hurt you as a newborn. Well look at the positive side. Without that nurse you'd probably not have the gift of speech or feeling.

Our dependency on others begins at conception and continues until even after death. Before conception you depend on your parent's desire for one another to create the environment where you can be formed. Before you are able have your first meal on your own, you depend on your mother to feed you. Prior to taking your first steps you depend on someone to hold your hands. Before your first words, you depend on someone to be speaking to you so that you can memorize the sounds and imitate them when the time comes for you to start to speak. On your deathbed, you need people to help you through your weakest moments as you engage in battle for your life. Even after you die, you depend on people to bury your remains, grow and water flowers at your grave site, as well as light candles in your memory. Although you're dead you still have people that are more than willing to carry on your legacy. What makes you think that you don't need your connections now?

Honorable John Olago Aluoch

This man appeared at the most crucial moment in my life and has remained a father figure in all aspects of my life and success. John paid my college school fees to pursue journalism and communication and supported me all through my studies. According to him, I was very ambitious. He'd never seen such a determined young lady before and was compelled to support my dreams. As a lawyer with a successful career in Kenya and abroad, he introduced me to his elite connections in my city. He was an example of success, humility, and a confirmation that dreams really do come true. After a few interactions, I started to think like the elites within his small circle of friends. I wanted more from life and would stop at nothing to get there. John hasn't just been a blessing to my modelling career, profession and family. He's remained my mentor, advisor, and the flame that keeps the fire within my dreams alive. I respect him and he shows me respect. Just like my late father he's constantly proud of my achievements in life and always willing to support me in any way possible. John has served two terms in the Kenyan government as the Member of Parliament for Kisumu and he still inspires me to obtain more from my life. Destiny connectors like John are ones that you should never let go. He's not just a past inspiration but full of inspiration today and even in the future. I'm blessed to have such a selfless individual as my mentor and friend.

The biggest challenge many face is keeping their friends or destiny connectors after they've achieved success. Some feel they've outgrown those relationships, based on the ladders they've climbed in life. However, you may still need these people. Let's see how we can keep a relationship going with your destiny connectors in the following pages.

Express gratitude

At times all our destiny connectors want to hear from us is, ''thank you for being there for me through my journey, it meant a lot to me.'' They don't need a new purse, suit, shoes, expensive jewelry or all those things you think you can give them to buy their existence in your life. Is a lack of thank you, worth losing a friend that's of so much importance to your destiny?

Create time for your friends

When you win an Oscar, I know you'll meet new people and these will want to steal all your time from the friends you had prior to winning that Oscar. Sometimes our new friends will mostly display themselves as most wanting of our relationship with them as our older ones. This is where we need to come to our senses and ask ourselves how these people survived before we came into their lives. Did they just dump their old friends for us and now expect us to dump our own for them? They've just showed up in our life after success. Will they stand by us when we aren't successful, as our older friends did? I'm not saying that you don't need to make new friends. I'm simply emphasizing that you create time for your old and new friends alike. Discover a balance and don't just lean on one side because you may be neglecting people that will later have a much greater impact on your future goals.

Authenticity

This is the number one illness most people suffer from after achieving their goals and becoming successful in life. People tend to forget the truth about their origins, the attributes that make them stand out from others, the commitments that once pushed them to pursue their goals in the first place, their sincerity to themselves and others, the devotions to themselves, their families, friends, and organizations, and the good intentions they once had for their goals and life in general. It's important that we stay authentic before, during, and after experiencing success. *A man that lacks authenticity is a slave of the other man he is imitating. He wallows in a hollow pursuit from which he can't achieve even a pinch of contentment.* Most of your friends will love to relate with you even more when they realize that you've maintained your image after being successful in life. Nobody I know or have ever met appreciates fake people as friends around them. Keep it real and your friends will stick with you. Lose your authenticity and watch the wind blow away most if not all your relationships in life.

Forgive and forget issues

When I was growing up my mom brought a few wall hangings with many helpful quotes. If you turned left or right in her house your eyes would always see a quote. One of my favorite ones was, ''some give and forgive, others get and forget.''- Unknown. Giving and forgiving, rather than getting and forgetting, is one of the teachings that has helped shaped my life. As brief as that saying may be, it carries volumes of wisdom that's highly relevant to our everyday life. In reality, the people we love will hurt and that includes our friends, frenemies, and destiny connectors. You remember those negative destiny connectors that we talked about in chapter two? Those mean friends who can't see your vision and almost prevents you from following your dreams? This is where you need them but you can't relate to these people unless you decide to forgive them for the pain they once caused or are still causing you and also forget all those troublesome moments.

Accept and apologize

Ego breaks even good relationships that could have flourished. This disconnects us from our destiny connectors and later limits our chances of learning or tapping from the wells of such wonderful people in our lives. If you've done something wrong, for the sake of relationships you need to accept that you made a mistake. Apologize to your friends and let them know that you're willing to work on your mistakes instead of blaming others for the things that you did wrong. It doesn't matter even if your friends' mean actions led you to doing that hurtful thing. You still need to apologize. I've often heard people say that they can't stoop so low to apologize to a particular person. They feel that they're so much better than that person, who they consider to be inferior. Well this isn't an attitude that builds anything, it breaks everything! All it does is break your relationships and before you know it you'll have nobody in your circle and you'll find yourself wanting to take yourself out too, just as you did your friends. Don't let your ego stop you from enjoying the benefits of destiny connectors. You need them today, tomorrow, and forever.

Keep your promises

There are so many relationships that have been ruined by a partner failing to keep their promises. Maybe you thought that only marriages suffer from this but even friendships with no sexual feelings involved, face similar suffering. Perhaps you promised to hang out with your friends after a very busy day. If your friend asks you to hang out with them on a specific date and you accept to do so, make it a point to honor that promise. We all know that emergencies can occur after making such plans. If that happens, remember you can't stop an emergency situation but you can notify your friend about what's happening and follow up with an apology stating that you regret not being able to connect that day. If he or she is a good friend, they should hear you out and not take any offence. Of course friends don't like you to cancel invitations on a regular basis. If you keep passing, they'll not include you on their list again, so whatever you do, make sure that you don't turn down all the invitations from friends. Make an effort to accept a few, if not all, of these invitations. If you keep turning them down, many friends will assume that now that you've tasted success at your and you've decided not to hang out with them anymore because they're less important to your life, which probably may not be the case at all. My mom is particular about keeping promises, she says it shows that you respect others and respect give room for relationships to grow.

Be generous with your compliments

Show me a man who'll never stop to compliment someone and I'll show you someone that has complete misery, sorry, jealousy and loneliness in their lives. Humans are affectionate creatures and they constantly need expression of affection directed towards them so that they can show the same to others. Compliments are nurtured in a heart that's full of love for others to feel and see the capability in them. You can't be generous with compliments if you lack the springs that produce the same compliments in your soul. Most of these attributes are natural with others but some people need to get into the habit of doing them so that they can be a blessing to themselves and others too. All you need to do is stop for a second and tell someone that you love their dress, even if it's the ugliest dress you've ever seen, that you're impressed by their achievements, and just be nice generally. At times someone may be weighed down with issues in life and these words can encourage take off a big load from them. Ever noticed that the people who are mean with compliments are also very negative people in life? It shouldn't surprise you because the bible says that out of abundance of the heart speaketh the mouth. The souls of these individuals are not flowing in the abundance of compliments and positivity. How can they speak out what they don't have or don't know about? If you're not an individual who compliments others, start doing so soon. It makes you friendlier and many people will love to be around you regardless of your position in life.

Be honest in your dealings

I met a woman that told me how she had to end a relationship with a long-term friend. She realized that the friend wasn't being honest in her dealings towards her goal in life. Her friend had started pursuing fashion and design career. It seemed as if she was doing so well in the market. Many people were buying her clothes and attending her fashion shows, where she always showcased her newest designs. One day, the woman offered to help her designer friend with one of her upcoming fashion events. This was when she realized that a portion of a collection that the designer was planning to showcase were not her own work but clothing bought from a local clothing boutique. The tags had been removed and a few print patches had been added to them. The woman felt so ashamed that someone she'd considered a friend would do something like this. She opened up and told her friend that she didn't feel that it was right to take someone else's work and claim it as her own. To the woman's surprise the designer defended herself, claiming that it wasn't a mistake to buy clothes, rip off the tags, and add tiny patches to them. The

Capable You –Everline Aboka   [164]

woman walked out of that relationship. She knew that if she continued to be associated with her friend she'd have to start making similar compromises in life, something she didn't want to be part of her existence. Even if lying isn't a big deal to you, keep in mind that some people take lying very seriously. Don't just lie to keep climbing the ladder of success because even if your friends choose to stick around and not leave the relationship, the long arm of the law will catch up with you one day. You'll find yourself charged in courts of law with mistakes that you could have easily avoided in your life, so choose wisely.

Be empathetic

"If your emotional abilities aren't in hand, if you don't have self-awareness, if you are not able to manage your distressing emotions, if you can't have empathy and have effective relationships, then no matter how smart you are, you are not going to get very far."

Daniel Goleman

We have friends so that we can be there for one another in our lowest moments whether we're successful or not. Empathy is the state of not only understanding but also feeling the emotions involved in the other person's heart and acting in such a way that you remain a spring of peace, comfort, and joy in their lives. We expect empathy from friends and they expect it from us in return. Lifting each other's spirits results in lifting each other's lives. Those who enjoy close genuine relationships tend to have a much happier and joy-filled life. For us to experience success in our lives we will need such qualities to help us to stay positive and focused on our goals.

I was recently sharing my charity ideas with a few black women in my state. I explained how it pained my heart that most street children in Kenya are boys. Organizations working with children give more attention on girls, not realizing that they're creating an in balance in our economy, crime rates, and societal acceptance in the future. I went ahead and explained everything in detail but was astonished when two of the woman finally asked how parents could take girls to school but not boys. I realized that nobody was paying attention to my explanations nor had any empathy for those boys struggling to make a living from the streets. By then I realized that a person can't have empathy unless they understand someone's feelings. As I was talking about boys and girls it became clear that the only thing that these two women understood was that a boy and a girl could only be real in a family set up. The women missed the point that the specific boys I was referring to all lived on the streets as orphans, rejected and neglected by their communities.

Maybe you're wondering how you can include empathy in your daily life? All it involves is understanding that although you have sufficient food and clothing for yourself, there are groups of people who lack and consider such as comforts. You feel touched in your spirit and decide to share some of your food and clothing with them. Often people think that to express empathy you have to do something bigger than this. Let me remind you that you're doing enough already by participating in such simple acts.

Don't just do this kind of thing with strangers. Do it with your friends and enemies too. It's not cool to let friends face challenging situations by themselves while you watch and probably laugh about it. Know that today it might be them needing you but tomorrow the tables may turn and you could need them just as much.

Practice confidentiality

Confidentiality is another quality that if used wisely will help you keep friends and nurture relationships for a lifetime. Yet if abused you're bound to live in misery and loneliness because nobody wants to spend time with an individual they can't trust with their personal information.

At times you'll realize that someone in your circle is going through so much that they feel it's time to release all the pain by pouring out all their heartache, misery, fears, and troubles the minute that they encounter you in a mall. This is when you adjust your empathy and confidentiality gears from zero to the highest number that you can attain. It doesn't matter if your highest number is ten or a million. The point is that whatever you do, ensure that you help this person to feel like a human being again. Offer a listening ear, encourage without being biased and most importantly remember not to disclose anything about the confidential conversation to anyone else, either in points or details, since this will end up breaking your friend and the relationship you both share.

Maybe you're thinking that all the times you've not practiced confidentiality is because you didn't ask your friend to share their troubles and secrets. Yes, you're right, you didn't ask them to share the issue with you. Yet the fact that they trusted you enough to share what's in their heart is a reason enough for you to zip up your mouth and forever hold your peace. Whether you're successful or not, the rules of the confidentiality game are the same. Just don't say a thing about something that was shared with you in confidentiality, period.

Communicate openly

Whichever way you choose to communicate with your circle, always know that your listening and responding with care in a conversation does a great deal of justice to those you are conversing with. People will want to spend more time with you if you're always listening to them instead of you always wanting them to listen to you. Of course being too quiet might send them away too, so find a balance between the two. If you intend to pass on some information, it's important that you use a language that all your friends understand. Speak in simple terms and avoid using professional terms in conversations with friends. The moment that we allow our professional language to take over our speech we risk closing our circles for many but a select few that are part of our professions. This may not be helpful considering that on your way up the success ladder you may need all kinds of people to carry you through your destiny. I hope you don't cut them out but use language that is understandable to most people.

Maybe you want to tell your friends that due to some emergency you can't hang out with them. You need to keep it simple and precise, mixing things together by talking about that event and something else only brings confusion. Since this stirs anger in a few individuals you might just realize that these people wouldn't want to hang out with you anymore, let alone be willing to help you reach your destiny.

Be fair

Truthfulness, love and fairness are siblings. Each of them compliments and leads to the other. Once we have the first two, the third will come so easily. We don't need to be reminded about this. Our commonsense gears will automatically kick in at the moment that they sense that we need to use them.

Being loving to your family, friends and many others will lead to your truthfulness about everything around them. You'll correct them in love, to make them grow but not break them. You'll stand with them in their hardest times when they face various challenging situations. You'll then know how to express your concerns about their situations without leaning on either of the sides.

I've learnt to treat all my family members equally and this is true about my friends too. None of them is better than the other and as a result I've noticed that taking sides doesn't come naturally to me. For example when two of my friends are on a bad terms I might be called upon to mediate. Even though I know most of the strengths and weakness of majority of my friends, I won't use this knowledge to make any judgement against them in such a situation. I'll listen to both sides of their stories, preferably in their presence, and offer unbiased advice. Letting unfairness take charge in your circle is like setting a traditional grass thatched house on fire. The entire house will quickly burn down and leave you with no house of friendship or powerful relationships.

Let your friends be their own boss
Have you ever heard your friend's remark that they can't hang out with someone because they feel he/she is too bossy? Yes, nobody wants to be anyone's slave.

People want to take control of their lives and maximize their abilities in order to make their lives better. They hate it when a friend comes in and takes over their lives. Because this section of the book is concerned with your behavior after you're successful in life, I knew that I'd be doing you an injustice if I failed to mention something about letting your friends run their lives. You see, we all know that after being successful you have smelled the air that your friends haven't smelled yet, you have achieved something they haven't. You have bigger visions and dreams than they do but that doesn't mean that you have the power to control their lives by telling them what to wear, what to eat, whom to date and so on. At least let them be in charge of their own personal lives and a good part of their professional life. All you can do is offer suggestions in the form of pieces of advice but never take charge of their live. They'll soon flee from you.

I have a friend that always believes that she knows everything I want. She forces her ideas on me and in most cases what she wants is the complete opposite of my own desires. At times she annoys me so much that I go for six to ten months without a real conversation with her. Despite me telling her not to force her ideas on me or meddle with my life, she'll keep on insisting that she's right, not knowing that this makes me feel bad about our relationship. As it is in any other relationship, I want to be in control, at least with regards to the things that concern me. We go about this same dilemma and for some reason the cycle keeps repeating itself. My friend is too proud to admit that she's wrong and I'm too proud to let anybody take control of my life. Maybe you behave like my friend? It's important that you start respecting your friend's decisions about their lives because not everyone will stick with you as I have with my friend.

Stay humble

To get to a point where you view yourself of low importance takes more than just thinking it'll happen but starting to travel the tough journey of humility, which includes practicing humility, speaking humility, eating humility, and sleeping humility. Humility is learned, just as pride is. We're not born proud or humble. We acquire such traits and we make them part of our lifestyle.

Because humility is a virtue and pride is a vice, pride always seems to demand our attention more than humility does. It's up to us to find ways to teach ourselves how to remain humble and selfless and one of my greatest references is from anonymous Abbess below.

Prayer of an Anonymous Abbess

"Lord, thou knowest better than myself that I am growing older and will soon be old. Keep me from becoming too talkative, and especially from the unfortunate habit of thinking that I must say something on every subject and at every opportunity.

Release me from the idea that I must straighten out other peoples' affairs. With my immense treasure of experience and wisdom, it seems a pity not to let everybody partake of it. But thou knowest, Lord, that in the end I will need a few friends

*Keep me from the recital of endless details; give me
wings to get to the point.*

*Grant me the patience to listen to the complaints of
others; help me to endure them with charity. But seal
my lips on my own aches and pains -- they increase
with the increasing years and my inclination to
recount them is also increasing.*

*I will not ask thee for improved memory, only for a
little more humility and less self-assurance when my
own memory doesn't agree with that of others. Teach
me the glorious lesson that occasionally I may be
wrong.*

*Keep me reasonably gentle. I do not have the
ambition to become a saint -- it is so hard to live with
some of them -- but a harsh old person is one of the
devil's masterpieces.*

*Make me sympathetic without being sentimental,
helpful but not bossy. Let me discover merits where I
had not expected them, and talents in people whom I*

Capable You –Everline Aboka   [176]

had not thought to possess any. And, Lord, give me the grace to tell them so. Amen"

If you're experiencing any challenges when learning to be humble in your life, here are some guiding steps regarding how to make yourself humble in life.

Talk less about your success

"The biggest challenge after success is shutting up about it." - Criss Jami

How many of us can shut up about what we've achieved in life, especially if it's simply bragging and not adding any value to another person's life? Could you come to a point in life after success and creep into a room, stay there, and not let anyone know that you're there? It takes humility to sit in the back row with the no name fellows in the society, even after being offered a seat at the front row.

Every time I travel back home to Kenya, people have expectations about me. They think that I won't listen to their conversations. They feel that I can't sit down with them on the floor and enjoy some local meals. They expect me not to ride on motorcycles or bicycles and not even throw a slim mattress on the floor and sleep on it. Upon meeting me they experience the opposite of their expectations. They tell me that they'd expected to see a tall, sophisticated, and skinny lady. They usually end with a smile on their faces and say, ''I'm touched by your humility, Everline.''

I grew up seeing humility modelled in my house and as a result from the best, my parents Raphael and Anna Aboka. My late father was a selfless man and so is my mother. Growing up in the slums, we were neighbors with people who were just the complete opposite of my parents. They'd brag about their children's performance in school, their shopping spree plans and so on. I can remember my mother always just listening to them and saying ''good for you.'' Then the following day the neighbors would see my parents and the children leaving for our shopping spree.

"Did you plan that last night after we talked?'' they'd ask my mother.

"As you know," my mother would calmly reply, "you cannot plan anything with this big family overnight. My husband and I have been working on this for months."

This happened repeatedly and I kept picking life lessons from the woman with the most beautiful soul, my mother Anna Awuor Aboka.

Today I arrive in places and show no concerns about my titles at all. It seems that my friends brag more about me than I ever thought. Sadly they don't understand why I don't. The truth is that I learned that titles, body shape, or career achievement mean nothing if we don't show humility to others and create major life impacts on people's lives. Whatever exists in our hearts matters more than what is in our height, body shape, body size, and life achievements.

I've seen people that often talk about their success. They're stuck in a limbo mode where they can't get higher in their pursuit. They're so lost in talking about what's happened that they forget about paying attention to what they should be working towards.

Pride is a trap that keeps you from reaching your destiny. You can always change that by starting to talk less about the things you've achieved in life and invest more time in your future endeavors. See the best in other people around you too. Accept that things can't always just be about you in this life. You're not the only living creature in this world. We have billions and billions of other things worth talking about, so pick even just one of them as a topic to talk about. This diverts the attention from you for a while, we all love such changes most of the time. People soon get tired of hearing someone boasting about themselves and their achievements. It's annoying and very inconsiderate to your audience.

A while ago, a woman I met at an event told me that she'd been searching my name on google search engines to know more about me prior to the our meeting. She was amazed at my background, achievements in life, and future plans. The conversation continued and I reminded her that I was really humbled by everything that was going on in my life. She immediately distracted me.

"'You shouldn't be humbled by your achievements but instead be very proud of them. If I were you I'd be on another planet, my friends would change, I wouldn't talk to people like me (she considers herself to be a total mess and feels sad that I have spared my time to listen to her), I would drive specific cars, wear specific designer dresses, and hang out in specific joints in the city,'' she continued to rant as I stood there smiling at her while inside I was in shock of what people really think of doing after they get to destination success.

I let her rant about her vision then told her politely that I really appreciated her vision of my life. The only thing that was different was that I was not her, therefore how she plans to live her life of success is completely different to how I live mine.

Toward the end of our conversation, I tossed the ball into her court. I reminded her of how capable she is of achieving her dreams too. I encouraged her to go after them in the same way I have and still do. This woman and I have connected many other times in the city after this first meeting and she can't stop reminding me about how my personality and how I carried myself the evening we first met changed her life and how she aspires to look at the world as I do and not the way her distorted vision lets her see it. She's since learned that with or without designer clothes, life goes on. With or without the most expensive car model life goes on. There are so many other things in life that we can do without but that often blind us so be happy and remain a blessing to others, especially in your conversations.

Avoid incuriosity

"There are young men and women up and down the land who happily (or unhappily) tell anyone who will listen that they don't have an academic turn of mind, or that they aren't lucky enough to have been blessed with a good memory, and yet can recite hundreds of pop lyrics and reel off any amount of information about footballers. Why? Because they are interested in those things. They are curious. If you are hungry for food, you are prepared to hunt high and low for it. If you are hungry for information it is the same. Information is all around us, now more than ever

before in human history. You barely have to stir or incommode yourself to find things out. The only reason people do not know much is because they do not care to know. They are incurious. Incuriosity is the most odd and most foolish failing there is." -The Fry Chronicles by Stephen Fry

I can't fail to agree with most philosophers that the reason that we're not better than yesterday is because we've refused to take an interest in some of the things that could make us better in life. As a result we've closed the doors to learning such important aspects of our lives. The same applies to humility. We're proud because we have interest in being proud and have learnt so much about it and mastered it almost all our lives. It's said that it takes an individual twenty-one days to turn a habit into a character. Is three weeks such a big deal for you that you can't set it aside to learn amazing traits like humility? I'm so adamant about humility because one hundred percent of crimes and injustices exist because somebody, somewhere, is too proud to learn, too arrogant to forgive, and too unloving that they are killing fellow humans like them. Without humility we can't let go. All we want to do is kill and destroy others. We're in constant competition about who is better than who and why. If such energy was pushed towards making our world a better place that would be awesome. Yet pride is too proud of itself and will stop at nothing until it gets its way, even if it means killing innocent men, women, and children.

To you, the reader of this book, the world has already experienced too many injustices. You could be the one to open wide the door of rationality and embrace humility, acceptance, and forgiveness, just by learning how to go about it. Think about the Holocaust that occurred in Europe decades ago. Would it have happened if Adolf Hitler and his advisors had the humility that leads to forgiveness in their hearts? "Definitely not". Would the white people have taken black people into captivity and killed them ruthlessly in the black holocaust that took place in the United States of America, Europe, and many other places around the world where such injustices occurred? "Definitely not," if at all somebody had been humble enough to realize that being dark skinned doesn't make someone inferior while being white skinned doesn't make someone superior either. Look at the beheadings by ISIS, Boko-haram, and Al-Shabaab that are part our world today. Would this be happening if someone took the time to teach these brilliant young men, who seem to know how to plan and succeed in their ruthless actions, the importance of humility and forgiveness? "Definitely not". *Humility chooses to find solutions through dialogue and understanding but pride seeks to make more war by responding aggressively to a situation that's already on fire. Choose to be the one that learns about humility, its ability to calm situations down, and not catalyze them. Know that a humble man seems weak in the sight of the proud but that same weakness is his main tool for strength to save this universe from chaos.*

I challenge you to stay curious about the knowledge of humility. Aspire to acquire it and change our universe, we are all doomed if we don't find a way out of this mess.

Stay calm under provocation

Anger is rooted in the presence of our inner being that's always wishing to prove itself to know it all, to want it all, and secure that which it wants but doesn't deserve. Perfection is for the proud as the opposite is for the humble.

The moment you realize that you can't be right all the time, get everything that you want to be happy, that is the kind of realization that confirms that you're not only learning to compromise but taping on the gift of humility too.

Anger escalates to war but humility is concerned with finding and making peace amidst unfathomable chaos. The world is chaotic. A sudden change of weather or a traffic jam in the morning on our way to work can cause us to lose our cool. Yet we have to constantly make a choice regarding being the boss of our feelings and reactions. We can't let situations take over because in most cases when they do all hell breaks loose in an environment where the presence of a hell makes no sense at all. I've often made a decision to let my feelings not control me because they don't know how to choose the right environment to sell their ugly goods. So why do they think that I can trust them with my reaction in that wrongly chosen environment? Anger doesn't know that you're having dinner with the president when you scroll through your social media and see a negative comment about yourself. All it wants you to do is get to its level, lose your cool, embarrass your hosts, and other guests then it'll feel good.

It takes humility to ignore so much going on around us just for the sake of the peace and sanity of our future. We can't fight everybody and everything around us. As I've said before, we cannot live with the expectations that we will be the center of interest all the times. We are not the only ones in this journey of life, there are many other travelers around us, despite their travel challenges, they, face other challenges as well and often needs a shoulder to lean on. We should not just expect people to fulfill our needs but rather be willing to offer our kind gestures to others as well. People around us often need us as too, we all need one another. They need us to carry their day-to-day pain. They need us to help them through their daily struggles. Only humility can help one to respond appropriately to such a friend's need. When your friend is angry or has done something that you find annoying, try and feel the pain that caused him or her to do that and brush off your pain of being insulted. Your friend might be suffering from something that's been boiling inside them for a long time. Since they haven't had anyone to share their misery with, they end up being so sensitive that a tiny bruise to their ego turns the whole place some kind of a hell on earth. This should be when you fully engage your calmness gear, stay sober, and keep your cool until your friend calms down. Later you might learn that your friend may not have meant to hurt you but was simply sensitive about a personal matter that had not been disclosed to you previously.

Share your success credits
We can't take all the credit for everything and still claim that we're the most humble souls alive. Humility has nothing to do with greed but everything to do with being charitable, even with your life

achievements. Throughout this book we've been looking at how one needs other people to push their wings higher, to enable them to get into the flying mood. Unfortunately you'll still hear me rant about this until the end of this book. You can change the story and say that you got to where you are by yourself. However, in reality some people won't forget those simple little things they did for you and even if you choose to forget, you should never forget what people did to guide you toward your success.

There may be people who did something such as ironing your shirt one day, serving or cooking you a meal, encouraging you, or supporting you financially, even in a small way. Perhaps they bought you a pencil or exercise book, took your clothes from the line so that they weren't rained on when you were busy or running late, brought you a cup of coffee when you were rushing to an interview without breakfast, or called you to join their family for dinner when you were far away from home chasing after your destiny. These people are all worthy of acknowledgement. When you finally see your star shining, don't forget them and keep all the credit from them, for you never know how soon you'll need them again.

When you celebrate that big award mention them. Even if you can't mention all your friends' names they'll still be happy that you remembered that ''friends'' aspect. It makes them feel part of your success and that they can share the joy with you, even if they are far away. There are times when I've thanked even my enemies for being against me. I've dedicated some awards to them as well because without them behaving like monkeys, pulling me down and preventing me from grabbing those yummy ripe bananas at the furthesr top of the banana tree, I wouldn't have salivated more for those yummy ripe bananas, they meanness kept me moving until I acquired some of my own ripe bananas from the banana tree. Always acknowledge your monkeys when you get your bananas. And when you're up that tree please grab them a few more bananas too. They might love the taste of success, even though they were trying so hard to pin you down. This isn't a joke. I'm as serious as a woman who just went into labor and is pushing that baby beside the road before she reaches the hospital.

My mother - Anna Awuor Otieno Aboka

As I write, I must acknowledge people who have made a huge contribution to my life. My loving mother's contribution to my communication skills. She was born in Kampala, Uganda, where her parents were successful business people. Just after her third birthday war broke out in Uganda and her family was forced to move back to their homeland in Ugenya, Siaya Kenya. Four years after their return to Kenya, her dad passed away leaving my grandmother with five children to care for, including a set of twins. My mother was the eldest of the five children but was still only six years old. My mother's memory of her childhood revolves around going to school for one term but if a relative needed a babysitter my mother would have to go with them to help out. She lived with relatives that treated her as a house help before she was barely ten years old. My grandmother was struggling to keep the five children together. The twins were often sick, forcing her to seek some help from her relatives. Many offered to help in return for household services performed by my mother and her sister, Josephine the second in their family. On several occasions my mother's relatives made promises to my grandmother that her two first girls (my mom and aunty Josephine) would go to school like the children of the households where they worked as babysitters as soon as they picked them up from their home. These promises were never honored most of the time for my mom but her sister Josephine experienced brutality in a relative's house in Nairobi, Kenya and still managed to go through the final years of her elementary schooling through such hardships. My mother was the smartest of her siblings and wished to go to school so much that she sometimes took the baby she was sitting into class with her. She struggled through almost to the finish line of elementary school but was later sent back to her own mother, where she joined school again. However, her uncles demanded she quit school and help one of her mother's sisters in Alego Siaya. My mother had no choice but to set off again. At that time nobody understood the importance of educating a girl child in Kenya. A few years later, she met my father, who was one of her aunt's neighbors. He was visiting from Nairobi where he was already working. They fell in love, married, had wonderful babies, and lived happily ever after until death took my dad away in 2003.

My mother's upbringing, in which she missed so much of her childhood, would later equip her to give my siblings and me the best childhood experiences we could ever ask for. Despite being so busy with her various businesses to supplement my dad's income, my mother still found time to clean us, cook for us, clean our clothes, take us to church every Sunday, made sure we all went through our catechism classes in church, got baptized confirmed and took part in the holy communion. She checked our homework, and made sure we were well behaved by regularly checking with our teachers. Some of my fondest memories are related to the nights when my mom sat us together to narrate to us various Luo fairytales ''sigana.'' Little did I know that my mom was building our listening skills, public speech capabilities, and writing skills. My siblings and I can clearly tell you today that the first teacher in our lives was our mother. Her stories had different topics that covered sex education, various virtues in life, and Luo cultural practices. This class was fun. We enjoyed it, always looked forward to it, and it strengthened our bond as siblings and with our mother. Today none of my siblings is shy about any aspect of their lives, even though some of us are introverts and others extremely extroverted. Yet one thing remains the same about us all. We can all explain ourselves and express our minds to others. We have lots of knowledge concerning many subjects that we didn't get from school but learned from our mother. We're all dreamers, just like her. We aspire that our children will get better treatment in life, just as our mother wished for us.

My mother was lucky that all her children have the best learning capabilities. We were all performing very well at school and our youngest sibling is also in his own league in this regard. One day in class seven I wrote a wonderful composition and my teacher marked it as 45/50. It wasn't easy for any student to get 40/50 in English composition in our class but I scoped 5 marks more above the unachievable. I went home and my brother Nick was so proud that I'd scored such an amazing grade that he took my composition with him to work. He was offering tutoring services to my neighbor's children of the same age as I and challenged them to write the same composition. Nick later came home and spoke to me. "Nyarber (beauty), out of this neighborhood no child of the same age as yours and the same grade as yours can write anything better than you. Can you believe your work is better than some student's in grade eight and nine too? Finish school and go to Britain and speak the Cambridge and Oxford English because that is where you belong."

Well, I know he was being extremely proud of me as my big brother and the best thing is that such memories still wake me up from my bed and make me want to write again and again. After many years I've stopped using the ambiguous Cambridge and Oxford vocabularies in my writing because I realize that my writing is mainly revolving around self-help.

I'm targeting a group for whom English is not their first language so for that reason it's important that I keep my words as simple as possible. I look forward to doing the same in my future writing as well as in my professional speaking events.

I hope to share a lot more about my mother in the near future. She's a woman of courage, determination, selflessness, and the epitome of dreams comes true when you work hard towards them. As of now, before I acknowledge my English teachers, the late Mrs. Okang, Mrs. Mukasa, Miss Idah Obondo, Mrs. Martha Oyugi of Central Primary School Kisumu Kenya, and the late Mr. Benard Nondi of Joel Omino high school, I would love to make it clear that it's my mother Anna Aboka who set this firm communications foundation and my teachers topped it up with excellent fertilizer. I honor my mother for such a wonderful gift, alongside my English teachers and any other individuals who played any part in helping me achieving the dream of being a writer, motivational speaker, and fashion model.

Treat others with dignity

Everyone wants respect. It surely takes humility that makes a person feel less important than others to be able to treat other people and himself or herself with dignity. People struggle to respect one another not because the other person is the devil, but evil lives in both their hearts. They haven't mastered the act of self-respect so respecting others becomes a cumbersome load. Whenever you hear a person ranting that others don't respect them and aren't treating them well, the chances are usually high that the victim doesn't practice self-respect either. They end up wanting that which they don't have. Respect isn't like money that you search for if you want some. Respect is nurtured within you. Don't expect it from others. Get it from within because that's where this beautiful magical river flows in abundance.

A good friend of mine is currently going through a separation with her husband of twelve years. A year before they decided to part ways, her husband said that he couldn't live in a relationship where he wasn't respected. His wife was surprised because she'd been dealing with a lot of disrespect from her husband and had decided to let him have his way all the time. With three wonderful children to take care of, a demanding job, and a husband, my friend was having a hard time keeping up with the constant pressures around her. Even though she still regularly attended her fitness and yoga classes, some aspects of her life had to endure a tremendous shift. As a result, she quit going out. She simply didn't have any time for it since nobody would help with their three children in the evenings and weekends. She dedicated her time to her husband, job, and the three children, one of whom suffered from cerebral palsy and always needed more attention. Little did this woman know that her staying at home was putting her at risk of depression. Soon she didn't want dress up, apart from when she went to work, and she quickly replaced her work clothes with pajamas after getting home. Her husband on the other hand liked to stay out late, drinking with friends, and arrive at midnight with lots of accusations against his wife. He started calling her names like ugly, stupid, bitch, fat and other negative words. He soon began to spend nights away from home and had an affair with his work colleague. He blamed this on his wife, who was also going through a hell of a time. He then separated from his wife and moved in with the work colleague, leaving his wife with whom he'd made vows of holy matrimony twelve years earlier, along with his three children.

One day I was talking to my friend and I realized that she was blaming herself for the demise of their marriage. I considered the way that I thought that she should look at this issue.

"Your husband had an affair with a woman when you were still married," I told her. "Then he went ahead and moved in with that woman, leaving you with the children. Your man has no respect for himself. He didn't respect the fact that he was a husband. He didn't respect the fact that he was a father that needed to be present for his children. And finally he didn't respect the vows of being there for both of you in better or worse moments till death parted you the two of you. The fact that he kept calling you names and claiming that you were disrespectful doesn't make you disrespectful. That's all he wants you to feel and see in you while the truth is that, he's the one who is disrespectful. He can't stand the act and is now passing blame on to you"

Where I come from, they say that "a thief likes to push claims that somebody has stolen from him, a witch likes to push claims that he has been bewitched" but it's all false. They're claiming what they're doing to others and then branding themselves victims of the same. This is my friend's ex-husband in a nutshell. You can brand it a shade of grey if you wish but ideally this matter of respect in their relationship is either black or white.

When you think respect, it's very mean to make it just about you, claiming that somebody doesn't respect you. Why not start respecting yourself so that you'll easily get it back. If this man thought about respect for his wife, marriage, and children, just for a moment, he wouldn't be so messed up by now. Ten months after moving in with his new girlfriend, he was kicked out when the woman got another man and told him that he wasn't a real man that she would date for a long time, let alone marry. It's hard to treat others with dignity but if you happen to be successful in this, rest assured that you'll be treated with dignity too in your life. You will get served the same meal you serve people around you, choose respect for yourself and others. You'll have long and lasting relationships.

Tame your ego

''While it is okay at times to see yourself as mighty, talented and all those positive attributes you feel only you possess and has a right to, also note that, there are people out there who have the same attributes or even better and when you considering the life of humility, letting go of such thoughts should take over those ever thirsty egos of yours, you cannot quench the thirst of your egos often and expect to be humble in life.''

There are people out there who have egos controlling them but they aren't aware of this. Others know that they have disturbing attributes but still consider these to be assets that aren't worth dropping. When friends notice that you have an ego, they'll just let you be and walk out because you don't build your friendships by claiming how big a god or goddess you are all the time. Your friends want and desire to see you plant positive things in their lives too. Egos break relationships because the ego always feels, things have to be done their way, and worst of all ego feels it has a right to make another person feel miserable. Even if an egomaniac was friends with a blind man, it would be so easy for the blind man to see clearly that the relationship was completely destructive and nothing whatsoever could come from it until the egomaniac replaced his ego with humility and love. In a world where there are many mysteries and none of us has evidence regarding the same mysteries, it's not right for one person to claim they know everything. Nobody knows it all and Albert Einstein didn't know everything either. All we can do is allow our imaginations to tell us what could be on the other side but not let our egos claim we know it all. We don't, we are constantly learning and wish to crack the mystery about topics like how we ended up on planet earth as human beings. Egos love to argue, about who is better, creation, source of life, the existence of God, life after death, who should make coffee in the morning, who should put the children in bed, or who should be blamed about many injustices around the world. On the other hand humility finds peace in enjoying the present sun, the existence of loved ones, the availability of peace, and the zeal to teach and share messages of peace with others. You can't prove people wrong by claiming that you know what you don't know. Over the years I've parted ways with people who feel that they know everything about religion, science and a range of other topics that breeds controversy and hate among groups. All I want is to enjoy my life in this universe while I still have the opportunity to breathe. I can't waste time, energy and emotions trying to prove what I can't prove because I have no evidence. I won't say that Christianity, Islam, Zionism, Buddhism, Sikhism, or any other faith is right or wrong because I honestly don't know and I don't want to waste any part of my life trying to prove this. It's beyond me as an individual. I only live with one assurance that there is a supernatural being somewhere, who is filled with love, care, and blessing for all. The more we show love to others, the more we'll easily realize the existence of God. Be wise enough to know that many groups out there are simply egomaniacs with one main agenda of winning many to their side and trying to outwit one another in a battle, using no evidences of their claims at all. Yet neither of them can win because they'll never have evidence to support their claims based on their misleading agendas, unless they change their agenda to start preaching and living by LOVE.

It's good to be open-minded and say that you don't know because you can't prove anything, but will wait and see, instead of claiming you know what you have no idea that you don't know. Many people find such attitudes annoying so simply tame your ego and stay open to the possibility that you don't know. At the time of the argument or discussion you may look like a loser or a lesser person for not knowing but in the end remember that the purpose of humility is to be less of yourself. Let's all begin to see each other as the wonderful beings we are. Let's operate in peace, love, and unity. Let's not allow various movements to separate us from one another so much that we can't shake hands or share a meal. Let's tame our egos and give back the sanity this world needs because we're the same. Color must stop separating us, religion must stop dividing us, and capitalism shouldn't define our class on this planet. We're the same from the North Pole to the coasts of Madagascar and we all have red blood flowing through our veins. Let's love and be loved.

Practice social intelligence

You exert social intelligence when you and everyone else know that you're the smartest but never refer to anyone or a situation as silly or stupid. You know that somebody has really hurt you but you choose to remain calm instead of picking a fight. You know that your friend is only needing attention by claiming that she's going through so much but you choose to encourage and uplift her spirit instead of judging her.

A toddler knows when its mother is annoyed and if she says ''sleep'' you'll see that tiny human trying to close its eyes and end up sleeping without giving it's mother a hell of time. On the contrary as adults we move from this state of knowing the right thing to do in such circumstances but let our arrogance take over. We let arrogance prove to our oppressors that they're wrong and as a result we pick a fight and making a bigger mess of the situation that wasn't close to being a slight problem. If arrogance blocks our highway to social intelligence then we must first desire to run over and kill that arrogance before we can proceed to social intelligence. Once again, note that it takes a great deal of humility to realize that we're arrogant and desire to act towards change.

A socially intelligent man may look weak, unconcerned or even disrespectful when he overlooks circumstances that are likely to escalate to a big fight. However, his calmness sets him apart from his counterparts that are constantly seeking war and in the end he gains so much by choosing the high road. This is how he matures and builds relationships around his life.

When I was growing up, my siblings and I heard our mother constantly remind us to think before we said something out loud. We were warned from talking as if the wind was forcefully opening our lips. We were to avoid saying some things even if we felt that we needed to say them. This was her way of making sure that all the seven of us were well behaved, around her and my father, in school, and around everyone else. She wasn't telling us to be well mannered, but how to be intelligent socially. Even at my current age when I'm faced with situations and want to react, I'm reminded of how that would hurt my mom. I realize that if that reply or comment would hurt my mom, then it would hurt someone else too, including me in the long run.

This concludes our ways of staying humble as a virtue that can help us while we're on our way to success and when enjoying that same success. I hope that you took some helpful information from it and that you'll not only aspire to bring change to your life but to also start acting toward achieving that same change.

Invest more, spend less and maintain a simple lifestyle

Not many of us come from backgrounds that encourage saving or investing. If you do, count yourself lucky because majority of the world's population doesn't know anything about investing until they're in their late thirties. Others die without a single investment in their life.

On the other hand, we're natural spenders unless you're an accountant. These are the only people I know that don't walk into a store and buy something just because it's affordably on sale. Yeah, that perfectly describes my brother, Nicholas. Some people have a way to save for something even before making a purchase. Others spend more than they make on a monthly basis and if you live in the developing world where credit history is a necessity when you want to own a car or even a house, you have no option but to have a credit card to help you build your credit history. The problem looms in when you're forced to use that card so that it equals your monthly income and end up without any part of your earnings being invested in another areas. A while ago I took some financial literacy classes and I realized the reason why we don't invest, spend more, and save nothing is because we all want to live a lifestyle that even millionaires can't afford. I was astonished to learn that billionaires like Bill Gates only purchase a few things for themselves each year. This is a man you would imagine owns 365 pairs of trousers, one for each day of the year but in fact he reuses his pair of trousers a couple times over twelve months. Someone like Bill Gates learned to invest first. After many years Microsoft has been successful and the man behind it is now mostly working on eradicating disease in third world countries. Isn't that just amazing?

Building wealth isn't part of our formal education system, likely because nobody in the government wants you to get that information. That's when you should go beyond school knowledge to extract more from of your work, talents, and time. The only thing that we're taught in school is to save money in a savings account. However if you investigate further you'll realize that the promised interest from the bank when you save your money is very little when compared to investing the same amount of money in a project that yields you even more money. A while ago I visited my bank. I wanted to save some money and from the amount that I was going to deposit the bank would give me $27 in interest but with conditions that I leave the money untouched for six month, if not, I got nothing. As the teller explained this, I told her that it was ridiculous considering that they were going to use my money to obtain more money for themselves. Following this experience I embarked on a journey of money literacy and am glad that I've been studying more about money than I ever did before. On that journey I met so much knowledge that has made many successful entrepreneurs stay on top of their game and a few of them are as listed below

The twelve commandments of the wealthy

We all want to be wealthy and when talking of wealth I'm referring to the individuals who are rich to the core in these times, such as Bill Gates, Carlos Slim

Helu, and Warren Buffet. The likes of Oprah Winfrey and Amancio Ortega. To be like these people, we have to learn how they operate and follow suit, think how they think, and see money as they see it. This will entail resetting our money mindset because for as long as I can remember as a Christian I thought that being filthy rich was a sin thanks to the stories of the rich man and Lazarus' as well as Judas Iscariot's betrayal of Jesus Christ, as told to me as a child in Sunday school. It's taken me years to eradicate that kind of programming from my mind and I now accept that money is not evil but good. It's what you do with money that can be either evil or good. You'd rather be filthy rich than filthy poor because when you're rich, you have a powerful tool to address issues affecting your society. Money can help to bring solutions to disease, homelessness, and poverty. Think about it. If someone's homeless and needs money for housing, yes you can pray for them but then God will need to touch somebody with money in order to provide the funds required to build a house for that homeless person. So do you see the value of money? Money can be a force for good when used wisely to improve lives and not oppress people.

However, it would be needless of me to share all this advice about it with you unless you change your mindset about money. Maybe all you know is about money is ''spend less and save more'' The time has come for you to revise your thinking with ''spend less and invest more'' if at all one of your dreams is to have financial stability. If your parents didn't leave you with that for your children and future generations, purpose to make it happen for you.

After reading and following the conversations of the filthy rich around the world I realized that none of them was born wealthy. Some were poorer to the core but the following provides a good insight into their dealings, investments, wealth and what they did to acquire such wealth.

The wealthy believe in constant learning
The successful and wealthy men throughout history have believed in constant learning. In fact when they

realize that they're the smartest in their circle, they simply walk out of that environment in pursuit of intellectual arousal in a far more intellectual team.

Considering that the majority of them have no higher learning knowledge, they still pursue this but not as a consumer would. Many people go to school to learn. However, our formal education system doesn't teach us much about investments, or the tricks and the means to secure a successful future with our investments. Such information can only be found in the circles of the business elite, or at seminars or workshops where the best of the best in the marketplace share the knowledge that has helped or is helping them grow on their journey. The wealthy spend much of their time traveling around and attending such powerful seminars and workshops around the globe.

The wealthy rise early

During my kindergarten years, my teacher would make all the students sing a song when we first arrived in class each morning and a few minutes before leaving for home. The song's lyrics were as follows:

"Early to bed and early to rise, make some men healthy and wealthy and wise'' - Unknown artist.
For my teacher, this song reminded us to go to bed early and also rise early the following day. As it has turned out, this song has remained my favorite and serves as a constant reminder in my life that to achieve success one must learn to go to bed early and wake up early too. In a society where partying all night, watching movies, and working very late night shifts has taken over sleeping at night, it's certainly a challenge to wake up early each morning. Yet once you decides to prioritize and make wise choices in this regard it's still possible to rise early.

Adequate sleep is crucial to your health, productivity, how you understand complex information and also plays a role in wealth creation. It's very important that you teach yourself the discipline of saying no to partying or watching movies all night and all other activities that prevent you from getting enough sleep.

Over the years I've noticed that I go to bed by nine o'clock in the evening and am mostly awake by three in the morning. Depending on where I am, I'll jump out of bed and engage in some meditation right after waking up. This helps to calm me in the morning and depending on the intensity of the day, I would read a book and enjoy my breakfast without a rush. There is something unique and sweet about waking up early before the birds and everybody else. The silence of that calm and serene hour sends you to a beautiful world of imaginations where you are likely to gain much from your inner being. I've developed this tendency since my elementary school days when I'd go home with mountains of homework and my mother would insist that I sleep early and wake up earlier in order to finish the task before leaving for school. It worked out perfectly in those days and as I moved into adulthood my mind refused to let go of this habit. Each time I overlook my routine and go to bed later at the night, I realize that I wake up at three in the morning or later but with a severe headache and altered mind. This will end up controlling my day instead of me controlling the day. It's no wonder that the song stressed that going to bed early makes one healthy, wealthy, and wise. If a lack of rest can make you feel unwell then it can also interfere with your productivity. This in turn will impact your wealth creation ability. Borrow this concept of rising early from the wealthy. It will make you healthier, wealthier and wiser than you are today.

The wealthy have an investor mindset not a consumer mindset

I may need this entire book to explain this aspect about the wealthy. However, since that's is not keeping with the harmonious flow of this plan, I'm going to share the basic details about this. If an individual with an investor mindset has $1,000, the first thing that he'll consider is investing this money into a business that will eventually generate double, triple, or ten thousand times the amount in return. If an individual with a consumer mentality has $1,000, he or she will either spend the money but not on anything that will bring in more returns. Or perhaps put the money into a savings account, which we all know has a very small percentage of return and mostly after a long period of time. I've never seen any of the wealthy people I've interacted with saving their money. To them money steps into the doors of a bank account and leaves just as quickly in order to be dropped into another investment to generate more money. They call this process letting go of the money to bring in more money.

The wealthy invest when the market is low and when the market is high

This is the number one aspect and as a young woman in my twenties I want to master as soon as possible. It's a philosophy that's both scary and confusing yet one which the rich in our society have mastered in order to create even more wealth for themselves. You see every time the government makes an announcement that the country is facing a two percent rate of inflation, every other Tom, Dick, and Harry goes into a panic mode, cutting all expenses and saving as much as they can. When they do this, they don't realize that they're actually putting the already rotten economy in jeopardy because economy's growth depends on the circulation of money for it to remain stable. As the economy worsens the consumers end up selling their cars, properties, and many other possessions that require monthly payments, believing that "the economy's in the toilet, so they can't afford to have a car type or their house." This scenario creates a very fertile ground for an investor to buy such possessions and houses at a very low price. These will then later be sold for triple or even the quadruple the amount they were purchased for, once the economy stabilizes. This works magic, especially for the prices of houses and lots, which tend to greatly appreciate over time.

The wealthy are their own boss

"Everline," a young millionaire once told me, "I can't work for anybody. It's a waste of my time, my capabilities, and natural resources while in return the compensation is even more of an insult."
Over time I've come to realize that the freedom of an individual's time could actually lead to their financial freedom in life. As an employee, you can't be in control of your employer but the opposite is very true. If he or she says that you must show up at work at the

weekend while he or she takes a vacation to somewhere warm because there's a freezing blizzard coming that weekend, you'll have to comply or possibly lose your job. Yet you can't even take a day off to baby-sit your two-year-old daughter before a replacement employee fills your position.

Coming to think of it, as someone that's always sought full time jobs working forty hours a week, I realized that forty hours is a very big investment in one's business and as a result I have made a big change of investing more time in some other activities that bring even much better rewards my way.

The rich know that time is money and they'd rather spend that time bringing in money for themselves than doing it for someone else.

The wealthy trust their instincts

To return to the importance of decision-making, the rich tend to have a lot of decisions to make in a short time. To simplify this process, many have told me that they decide what to do about most issues as soon as they encounter such issues, they have no second to waste belly dancing upon issues. This is because if they procrastinate when it comes to making decisions they're prone to fail doing any business which could lead to facing loss of many of their businesses and clients. The success of their decisions is based on that very first instinct that they feel when a business opportunity arrives. For example, if this instinct leads to the acquisition of bigger profits after investing $500,000 then they go for it. If their instincts tell them the opposite they'll definitely not invest in that business. The rich say that sometimes their instincts are wrong regarding the outcome of a particular investment but at that point they stay positive and dwell on the fact that they made a decision. This is because failure to do so would still produce the same result. The failure to make such a decision at that point could be itself considered making a decision.

The wealthy are entrepreneurs not technicians

An entrepreneur mentality allows a businessperson to devise a system that allows work to go on at the company in the presence or absence of the director or owner. A technician mentality allows the business individual to do everything alone so that if the owner is absent the business is inoperative until the owner returns. The entrepreneur mindset gives the rich the ability to not only make money through the various employees of the company but also find time for other important things, such as spending time with the family, or engaging in a sporting activity. To give you a better insight into the company of a rich entrepreneur you'll find a full-time security person, receptionist, accountant, and a human resource manager, all the way up to the director that may also be the owner. However, a technician doesn't have any employees, so he or she does everything, isn't that productive, and therefore doesn't bring much income into the company.

The wealthy borrow money constantly and use it wisely

Another characteristic of the rich that blows my mind is their positive attitude to borrowing money from banks and other sources. In their transactions, you'll see a millionaire receiving a cheque for more than a million dollars but you'll still see him or her calling the bank requesting money to use in a new investment opportunity. You might wonder why the millionaire doesn't simply invest a portion or all of that check, such individuals can't do that. The new cheque will be deposited only to reach a maturity date. As soon as that's done the money is released from the account so that it can bring in more money. Creepy perhaps, but that's the reality of a millionaire's daily transactions.

The wealthy bloom where they're planted
Remember the late Steve Jobs? This was a man that seemed to have had all odd against him right from his conception but became one of the most celebrated investors of all time. I can't fathom what it must have meant for a little boy who's biological father, a self-made Muslim millionaire and whose mother had to plan a secret adoption of their son to non-college graduates Paul and Clara Jobs, simply because his maternal grandparents wouldn't allow their daughter to marry a Muslim man, even though they were in love and expecting their first baby. Steve then grew up in a household which initially his mother didn't

want him to live in but finally signed the adoption papers when Paul Jobs agreed to go to college. Steve started Apple in his parents' garage. What I'm driving at is that this man knew that all he had to do was bloom where he was planted. He didn't sit down and say that because his biological dad had so much, he wasn't going to work hard. No, Steve Jobs went on the build a multi-billion dollar company still admired by many today.

Wealthy people embrace failure

Although failure isn't embraced in most households, this doesn't mean that every failure is bad. Failing simply means that you're out there, pushing yourself beyond your limits. Even though you know it's not an area where you can immediately succeed, you keep pushing yourself and that's the biggest key to success. How will you know you can do something if you don't try?

"You can't measure failure of a task not performed, let alone the success of the same task."

It's wise to go out there and attempt something that you wish to try out but are still afraid will end in failure. It's time to invest in that business, talent and whatever you're interested in right now now without allowing your fear of failure to control you. Turn that fear of failure around and anticipate success.

Consider failure as a lesson, not a death sentence. In every failure there's a lesson to be learned if you look closely. Without failing you can't learn about some aspects of life. Failure is a recipe of success, so don't deny it a place on your journey. You need it to see the other end of your success.

Wealthier people stay in the circle of the wealthy
The rich take the saying ''birds of the same feathers flock together'' very seriously. They also know that energies are transferable and want the right kind of successful energy to be transferred to them. The people you constantly spend your quality time with will reflect on your character, finances, marriage, children, spiritual life, health, and fitness.

If there's one thing that we can learn from the wealthiest 1% it's the importance of keeping the right circle around us. I'm not suggesting that you should call all your friends and make an announcement that you're leaving their circle because you've achieved something that they haven't. All you need to do is be wise about it. Slowly detach yourself from people that you believe are going to hinder your growth toward success. You don't need to hang around their negativity on a daily basis and you don't need to meet with them regularly over coffee. Yet there are some friends that once you realize their role in your life and mission to success, it'll only do you good to meet them on Christmas Day, when everybody is so immersed in a merrier spirit, including them for that one day when they forget about criticizing your dreams. Don't give me that look, my dear reader! I just gave you the coolest tip right there!

Wealthy people never seize an opportunity

This is something that I've practiced for some time now and I'm glad I do it. There are some people who spend so much time analyzing an opportunity, considering all the reasons why they shouldn't take it. They think about how their husband, wife, children, friends, church members, parents, or siblings might feel hurt if they took part in that opportunity. Interestingly, the last person they think about in these circumstances is themselves. This makes it a weird situation because if an opportunity presents itself to you, you should first consider how it might potentially improve your life better before you think about hurting others just because their hearts are probably filled with jealousy. For the record, the kinds of opportunities I'm referring to are those that are supposed to make you a better person, make our universe a better place, and help us impact the people around us in a positive way. I'm not talking about making atomic bombs, nuclear weapons and things like that.

I recall the look I used to get from some of my very judgmental religious Christian circle when I started modelling. To them modelling was worldly and wasn't something that a devoted Christian lady like me should be pursuing. One day at home, I noticed that I lacked many basic needs that my accusers couldn't provide me with even though most of them had so much. That's the day I made a decision to never seize any opportunity. I realized that at the end of the day they'll condemn me but can't provide for me. I was the one who had to deal with the pain of their condemnation and those of my lack. I decided to create a strong bond within me, invited my conscience and instincts into this bond and from that day onward on I do as we (my conscience, instincts and everything within me) agree, no external parties are invited in our private decision making process.

The wealthy believe in profit

I'll bet that you're thinking that this refers to financial profit, but it doesn't just mean that. Rich people in our society work around the clock. Who'll spend time on something that isn't increasing anything for them? I wouldn't since that would entail doing more things here and there without a goal, making it difficult to know whether you're making profits or losses. When a company donates $10 million to a worthy cause, they believe that this will make them appear as an organization that's supportive of the community, which might bring them more business at a later date. I know what you're thinking but that's one of the most important marketing strategies for many big companies. Such organizations are owned solely or in partnership with the richest people around us. These people will do anything to keep the money coming in, more investors coming in, and more partnerships coming in, because this provides them with the means to create more profit thus more capital for other new investments or to boost existing ones.

Fundamentals of Investment

From my financial freedom and financial literacy classes, I've learnt that a penny in the pocket is better than a penny spent at the store. It's even better if a penny is invested and generating some sort of income. In a world where fluctuations in economies, and in the prices of goods and services are commonplace it's safer to find a way to have money coming in at a higher rate than it's going out. It doesn't matter how small you start or how little you make. That will eventually fill your storage pot. So how do we get that pot filled?

What to invest in

The most critical consideration about investing is determining what to invest in. This question also leads to others such as why, where and when to invest. I choose to invest in projects or businesses that are in line with my goals and principles because at the end of the day it shouldn't just be all about making money but also about improving lives. I know that most investors don't think this way anymore, but remember, you don't have to be like anyone else. You're distinguished among your peers to make good choices.

For example, if you care deeply about the problem of world hunger, you'll invest your money in companies and organizations developing solutions to food insecurities. This can involve funding agricultural research or supporting local farmers to cultivate crops that have higher yields. You could also establish a farm that grows crops for commercial use.

Of course you might not have large amounts of money for funding bigger projects. Perhaps you could consider poultry farming, even if the starting goal is to provide your community of 100 people with a steady supply of eggs and meat. How about clean water? In most third world countries there's often scarcity of clean drinking water. You could start your own project as I did in 2007 and sell tap water, even if it costs five Kenyan shillings for a twenty-liter container. In my experience the water project was not only profitable but also fulfilling. After conducting research in Nyalenda, I realized that the people in the community didn't have fairly distributed water collection points. The majority of the houses there weren't self-contained and lacked running water. Everybody used water every day so I knew that such a project would make money and also help the community. I was right. The members of the community were much happier that they no longer had to travel long distance to collect water. Bringing them clean, cheap water represented great progress. The water business is one in which I believe anybody can become involved in. After installing your tap, all you need is someone that can be near the water point to operate the tap for clients and collect their payments. Above all it's a non-perishable product that you pay your monthly bills according to the liters of water you sold that month. Mostly I paid 10% or lesser of my total earnings from the water sale on a monthly basis. The lowest sale points occurred on rainy days but it wasn't a loss for me because ultimately my bill payments depended on my sales. When considering your investments it's important that you're familiar with the benefits and risks of such investment, along with such things as related legal requirements.

How much and how often?

As I said earlier, you can achieve financial freedom by investing some money in a project. This may start small but in time it could blossom into something bigger. Knowing how much we put in an investment and how often this happens can help us determine if we're running at a loss or making progress. It's important to keep a note about this kind of information somewhere so that we can always go back and track it whenever necessary. Even if you prefer to save money to later earn interest on it, you'll still need to know how much to set aside for this purpose on a daily, weekly, monthly, bi-monthly, quarterly, annually basis, depending on what works for you.

Risks involved

Before you begin, it's important to know all the risks of an investment that you're planning to get involved in. All investments have a certain risk connected to them. Some investments have bigger risks and others have fewer. You need to identify a plan of action to solve the situation when the risk becomes clear and get out of it without losing all the time, energy, and the finances you'd previously invested.

Be patient

Everybody always seems to be in a rush to realize profits from an investment. This might take less or more time depending on the type of investment so it's important to be patient once you've started a project. We all know that hurrying rarely has blessings attached to it, so you don't want to sink your business by taking actions that you can easily avoid when you take it easy, stay calm and wait for the results of your labor to come to fruition.

Stay informed about your chosen market and look ahead

One mistake most investors make is failing to study their markets after investing. They also don't look ahead so that they can explore newer market after making the first investment. When you fail to stay informed about your market, you won't know whether the goods or services you've invested in will bring you benefits or losses. You could receive a surprise, which is great when it's profitable, but a very different story when it's a loss and you've probably lost everything.

For a poultry farmer in Kenya, it is obvious that business will be better in the month of December. Rearing more chicken from September to December is a very good idea, as opposed to doing that in January. That's because during festive celebrations most Kenyan households have a chicken dish on their menu. However in January it's totally a different story because parents are focused on taking children back to school. They're spending so much on school fees, uniforms, and books that the last thing most parents can think about is a fancy meal. Farmers that grow kale, spinach, cabbage and other cheap vegetables benefit more in January because parents still have to feed their families even as they minimize food expenses.

A poultry farmer that's looking ahead and planning to enter into other investment options in January could start planting vegetables in October. This would target the booming vegetable market in January instead of staying out of business because nobody would be buying chicken during that month.

Employ an investment broker

With the knowledge that some millionaires might read this book too, I felt it would be wise to give them a way to invest too. Not all millionaires have investments, right? Consider someone that's just been lucky and won millions of dollars in a lottery. They still need professional help. Someone that has a lot of money has no time and energy to go through the first five stages outlined above and could definitely use the help of an investment broker to handle the money matters on their behalf. This doesn't mean that you not do anything since brokers reduce your stress and the time you spend looking after your financial affairs. You'll still need to have at least weekly meetings to stay up to date and can even provide some input with regards to your investments.

Spending less

Most people who overspend never even realize that they do so until it's too late and they've become completely bankrupt. When you have money or a credit card, there's always an urge to purchase something that you didn't plan to buy when you walked into a store. The retail stores have also mastered ways of manipulating you into buying goods and services on a daily basis. They know that people are so impulsive and employ loopholes with campaigns such as red sticker days, 50% or 80% off one-day sales discounts when a store's closing down. After once working in the retail industry I realized that the retailers want your money and they'll do anything, including lying to you, to encourage you to spend money. They know that shoppers love discounts so they even increase the price of an item by 30%, but still put the new high price on a red sticker, place a poster stating 50% off on top of the product, and amazingly that product will sell like hot cakes on the day that the price was hiked, far more than it did at the regular price. From this experience, I learnt to buy items that weren't marked down but non sale items because often price markdowns are actually price markups Earlier this year I decided to spend less and realized where most people have difficulties in this area. I wanted to help others spend less and advise them where they could adjust their expenditure by making a few changes in certain areas.

Plan and cook meals

Growing up, I saw my mother plan family meals and I believe that this helped her to put her budget in place. She still does this today and it's an obsession passed down to me from her. Some people plan weekly meals while others do this on a daily basis. I've found that a plan's duration isn't that important. What matters is that there's a plan in place, which also acts as a guide to the type of food you eat, when, where you eat, and the person that prepares it. It's cheaper to buy groceries of $10 that could make a meal for the whole week than to spend $10 on lunch every day at work. If you work five days a week and cook your meals you'll end up saving almost $40 a week on lunches alone. If you include dinners and breakfast you could save even more. Let's imagine that you're the type of person that rushes out in the morning, runs to a coffee shop where you spend $5 on a cup of medium coffee and a doughnut, go to a restaurant and spend $10 on lunch and then in the evening you spend another $10 at a local restaurant. You're spending $25 a day. Yet for $25 you could easily make your own coffee at home, take your lunch to work, and eat dinner at home, saving $100 a week instead of spending $125 on food alone during the week.

Use up all items in fridge and pantry before your next grocery shopping

Because of the addiction of buying so much, many people purchase food items that expire in the pantry and are then thrown away. You can either live by the rule of buying your groceries weekly, without exceeding the required amount, or use up everything that stored in the fridge and freezer before going out to purchase more. This will save your household a lot of money.

Buy clothes and shoes only when needed

Last year, I realized that I had more pairs of shoes than the combined number calculated from the ages of my mother and all my siblings. I'd inadvertently become a shoe addict and the worst part was that I wasn't wearing some of these shoes at all. I realized that I owned pairs of shoes that I'd bought online three years earlier that I never wore at all. I was devastated, considering these shoes were very expensive. I made a decision not to buy more until all these shoes were worn out Nine months later I haven't purchased any more pairs of shoes and I hope

I keep up the good fight. When it comes to clothes, there's a simple rule. Only buy a few items that are necessary. You don't need to have everything that's in fashion. Don't be driven by what's in or not. As long as you can cover your body and look presentable, you're good to go. By the way, when I say buy only when needed, I don't mean that you should just purchase items when you feel like buying them! Everybody feels like buying a pair of shoes or clothing when they walk into a store but they don't need these things unless they walked into the store naked. Buy clothes and shoes when you have none. Don't be trapped in that womanhood cell of always claiming that you don't have anything to wear when your biggest problem in the house is the lack of space where you can keep all your clothing and shoes. Nobody can wear one hundred pair of shoes in a year, so why buy them?

Avoid designer brands

I see people who haven't got much money flinging designer bags, purses, shoes, and clothes left, right, and center. They keep building these big brand names when all they truly need is a functional bag, along with a dress, purse, or shoes. Why would someone spend $3,000 on a pair of shoes that you can buy for $10 somewhere else? People think that designer goods are bquality wise but the quality of most goods are the same. They're mostly made in China, India, Vietnam, or Philippines, right? Every company makes goods so that you can keep buying them. Do you think designer companies will be stupid enough to make a bag that lasts for a decade so that you won't go back to buy another one in the next few months? It's just the opposite. They want you to buy more of those products every season so don't be fooled. Buy functionality, not names because at the end of the day some no name brands are of better quality than the big name brands. Imagine buying a designer purse for 500 dollars and lacking even 10 dollars to carry in that bag, you might as well go buy a 10 dollar bag and keep the 490 in your cheap yet functional bag as you await to invest that 490 dollars in a profitable project.

Buy in bulk

Regarding items that you use regularly and in large quantities, it's safer to buy them in bulk than in small packages because this saves you money and time. A family of fifteen that uses sugar and rice everyday could consider buying 50 kilogram sacks of each, instead of running to the store for a two kilogram pack on a daily basis.

Stop buying bottled water

We all want safe drinking water, but seriously is it worth the price? In most cases we're buying a plastic bottle that we can't re-use for that ridiculous price. One might as well invest in a water bottle and a water purifying system to have clean and handy water all the time without having to continually invest in expensive bottled water.

Use cash

In Canada, the acquisition of a credit card is as good as using it. However, the only challenge with buying goods and services using credit or debit cards is that you can't track your expenditure on the go. When you have cash, you'll easily know how much you've spent in comparison to your last bank withdrawal as opposed to when you're continuously swiping those cards on those chip machines. Avoid using credit cards as much as you'd like to and only spend the money that you have on necessary goods and services.

Plan personal treats

Many people spend so much money on unplanned personal treats. It's good that you want your hair and nails to look nice but it's also important that you plan the frequency of using these services. It makes much sense to me as a woman to have manicure once a month and a pedicure bi-monthly. Hair appointments are a monthly expenditure and the occasional dinner is also an option when done once or twice a month. You can't expect to spend less when you go to the club every single day or on a weekly basis. That money being spent on alcohol all the time is only making you poorer and poorer. Your friends will come, you'll treat them as you treat yourself but you're the one with the huge credit card bill to pay at the end of the day so be wise.

Be a library darling

Many people spend so much money on books and entertainment. I know that in Canada you can get most books and many movies at the library so it's unnecessary to buy movies and music online to stay entertained. Check with the libraries around you too. Maybe all the books you need you shouldn't buy at all. Except this book ''Capable You'', this one you should own. Borrow other books, read them, and return them whenever you're done. Learning never stops. Even if you've never visited the library, go to one. You could acquire life-changing knowledge from those stacks of books in that big quiet building. Just try it because it's well worth your time, energy, and efforts.

Spend money on goods and services that build you

This is a little bit different from spending only when necessary but has more to do with spending money on good or services that build your career and talents. As a model spending money on shoes finally didn't result in such a great loss because as long as I'm still modelling I'll need these shoes, even for my own projects in the future. Attending professional writing seminars and boot camps is also a good way of spending my money. At these events I meet like-minded people who are likely to inspire my writing talent. I even meet with my mentors to determine if I'm on the right track as far as writing and book publishing is concerned.

If I were to spend thousands of dollars travelling to Hawaii with a group of friends to take part in a mission that's completely off my dreams and ambitions, this would be considered impulsive. This would also be risky for my financial stability and freedom.

Wait a few days before spending over fifty dollars
At times you might walk into a store and you realize that the one purse you've been looking forward to owning is now on sale. Instead of the regular price of $100 the purse is now only $52. That's more than a

40 percent discount and you can't wait to pay for it. This is the time when you should leave that store, running without that purse. Go home, take a few more days, and you'll later realize you don't even need that purse anymore. You'll realize that you have so many purses that you haven't used that you sincerely don't need another one just sitting around in the closet.

This is a little secret that can help you avoid spending. This isn't just for women but applies to men too and helps you avoid buying goods that you won't use. When you're in the store all that goes into your mind is, ''I need it, I need it now,'' but when you get home the whole situation changes.
You could use it once to the maximum but is that worth the $50 you spent on that item? Probably not, so just take your time and decide later. Don't just buy it right away.

Pay off your credit cards monthly
If you own a credit card, learn to pay off the credit you've accumulated on a monthly basis without fail. The bank wants you to have a credit card but they

also want you to pay interest and are always very quick to add a penalty once a payment has been missed. At least pay your minimum balance and if you can pay a bigger amount or pay off all that debt to remove it from your shoulders, go for it. I've heard of cases where people only had a $1,000 limit on their credit cards but since they failed to pay their usage on time, they ended up paying $5,000 or more to their banks. To ensure that you don't forget about credit payments, set reminders to alert you when the payment dates are approaching.

Community Involvement

After achieving a certain level of success, whether big or small, I find it more fulfilling and rewarding to start a charity organization or support an already established one that will address a specific issue or issues in the local community and society at large. Many people have solved various issues simply by taking this step to change lives around them. The best thing about charity organizations is that you affect the lives of others as well as your own. It blesses you with the self-awareness of not being self-centered but to think about others too. Even though success makes it's a little easier for one to start a charity organization, there are many that were built as a result of challenges that individuals went through rather than because of the success they achieved. You can make a difference in people's life even when your own life isn't perfect. I learnt this from my mother in the story below.

(The names are not the real names of persons referred to)
In 2005, Lydia and John were expecting their third child. Unfortunately their first two children had both passed away before their third birthdays. They'd known the pain of giving birth to sick children and nursing them to their death beds, which was a devastating way to start a family life. When the time came for Lydia to have her third child, she opted to employ a community midwife as she'd done with her two previous births. Even though she managed to successfully push out a healthy baby girl, Lydia emitted her last breath on her delivery bed as result of excessive post-delivery bleeding. To keep Lydia's

memory alive, her husband John decided to name their new girl Lydia. After the woman's burial, the baby's maternal grandmother decided that she would take the baby Lydia to the village to raise her since she was convinced that her son-in-law couldn't do that singlehandedly as a man. They agreed on father's monthly visits. John visited for six different times in six months. He would go and see his daughter at his mother-in-law's home with the child supplies, but wasn't allowed to touch or see the baby. His mother in law claimed that he had a few customary issues to take care of. One day John insisted on seeing his child so he took his own mother with him to see baby Lydia' on his behalf. To their surprise she was very sick but nobody had told them. It was at this point that John decided to take the child back with him to the house that he rented in town.

It's at this time that John sought my mom's opinion on his sick little girl and without wasting time, my mother suggested on taking the baby to our family practitioner, Doctor Oringi, who later advised that the baby should undergo a few tests at a local hospital.

The results showed that the little girl had full-blown HIV. This explained her low weight, the fact that every bone was visible in her tiny body that was covered with big boils, her constant fever, lack of energy, inability to move nor cry out loud, play or even eat.

All these took place when I was mainly a teenager and I saw a powerful quality that I still admire in my mother today. She stepped up and accepted responsibility for taking of the little Lydia. She took her to her daily, weekly, and later monthly appointments at the clinic. She cleaned and massaged, gave her medication, fed nutritious formula, and raised little Lydia as if she were her own child. Many people thought that she Lydia was my little sister. I remember when she stepped in to help many also told her to stop wasting time because the girl looked so frail and that she would die soon. Yet my mother saw hope and resurrection of life where most people didn't. She invested her love, time, money, and even dignity in the little girl. My mother woke up very early to take care of her business in the neighborhood to be able to walk twenty five kilometers carrying little Lydia on her back to make it to her clinic appointments on time. With time, little Lydia's health began to improve, the boils on her body cleared, and she stared becoming cheerful. She played and developed as a normal healthy child, while her body weight increased by each passing month. The little girl grew up knowing my mother was her mother and my family was her family. Lydia started going to pre-school a few years later. Today she's in grade three in Kenya's school system. Unfortunately her father passed away a few years ago and she was taken under the care of her uncle

My mother stepped up to care for Lydia at a difficult time in her life. At a time when she had just lost my father in 2003, then her mother in 2004, and had seven children to take care of, all by herself. Life had certainly thrown her a curve. You can only imagine the commotion she had in her head. Personally I can't fathom how she coped, but the fact remains that she did it and I'll applaud her forever for doing so. In my coming writings I'll share more with you about instances where my mother's actions have pushed me to become even a better person and how you too can change the world around you. Just as my mom you can step up to help a situation in your community as well. Make a difference, live better

www.ingramcontent.com/pod-product-compliance
Lightning Source LLC
Chambersburg PA
CBHW071601030726
47593CB00001BA/262